THROUGH THESE EYES

A Personal Journey From Catastrophe to Possibility

Clark Lord

 FriesenPress

One Printers Way
Altona, MB R0G 0B0
Canada

www.friesenpress.com

Back cover photo taken by a passerby. 2017, "The Pitons", St. Lucia.

ISBN
978-1-03-918260-8 (Hardcover)
978-1-03-918259-2 (Paperback)
978-1-03-918261-5 (eBook)

1. BIOGRAPHY & AUTOBIOGRAPHY, PERSONAL MEMOIRS

Distributed to the trade by The Ingram Book Company

Acknowledgement

Life, Mom, Tiffany, Athena, the taxi driver who stopped to call for help when he saw me lying unconscious in the street, Dr. Christian Ulic, Cheryl Bradbury, Ivan Rendulic, Daniel Carroll, lawyers, doctors, Nicole Meens-Miller, Ontario Shores, Danny Shannahan, Paul Bloomfield, Lyndhurst, St.Michael's, emergency workers, Ecu-Homes staff, Elke McLennan, Anne Cooper, police, Kathryn Meghan Mckernan, the Akiwenzie family, Adam Wagman, Dr.Milan Unarket, Mark Bruce, Steve Mezlenyi, Jeremy Lord, Saulis Tribinicus (Kingman), all the original Kensington massive, and others all along the way (too numerous to mention).

Thanks to all who said no, to all who said never, to all who said maybe. To all who said "Why", I say why not? Thanks to all the doubt, fear and illusion, you continue to provide a worthy adversary, constantly. You have been my Everest. Thank you to the liars and thieves, for lighting the path to truth and righteousness. Thanks to all.

Thanks to all the messages in the sands. The notes in the stars. The voice of the wind. To all the sideways glances, necessary to make it from here to there. To those that didn't need to ask, or who didn't need to BE asked. To all those that showed up at precisely the wrong and right moments. To all the right and wrong notes, that have choreographed themselves into the symphony of this moment.

Testimonials

"I've been with Clark since he settled his battle with the insurance companies. At that time, he was far from recovered. It has been amazing to watch him emerge from the ashes of catastrophic injury and financial fragmentation to rise above his disabilities, take the reins of his life, and charge forward."

Daniel K. Carroll, Senior Partner, Hudson Wealth & Trust Planning Group, Toronto, Canada.

"A must read for those seeking inspiration about strength, courage and determination at the time of adversity."

B. Cristian Ulic, MD, FRCPC Staff Psychiatrist, Mount Sinai Hospital, Toronto, Canada.

"Mr. Clark has been one of my patients since the early days of his journey. I have witnessed that he has endured many challenges but has persevered much adversity since I first met him 14 years ago. He should be commended for his ongoing efforts to better himself each and every day. I have no doubt that this book will be a valuable perspective to anyone who reads it."

Dr. Milan Unarket, Psychiatrist, Toronto, Canada.

"I have had the distinct unique experience of being acquainted with Mr. Clark Lord for the better part of 14 years. He has never ceased to challenge my concept of "reality", and its limitlessness, for this is what he aims to do with his inspiring tale. I dare to say that he hits the target!"

Ivan Rendulic, former Peer Support Coordinator, Spinal Chord Injury Ontario, Lyndhurst Hospital, Toronto, Ontario.

"Clark's story is one of incredible feats. His journey through life, the way he handles challenges, and his accomplishments are truly inspiring. His book paints a visual of the true strength in human resilience."

Stephanie Almedia, Made to Measure Specialist, Harry Rosen, Toronto, Canada.

"I have come to know Mr. Lord over the past few years. He has never failed to provide a unique perspective on the general state of affairs, or what they appeared to be. In this striking debut, he provides the reader with the opportunity to put this lens upon themselves. Don't hesitate in allowing yourself the possibility of sharing in this thrilling moment!"

Kalev Koop, Sales Representative, RE/MAX Hallmark First Group Realty Ltd. Ajax, Ontario, Canada

To the Reader:
It's Your Choice

To whom it may concern: this is a humble effort. An effort to pass on what it took too long to acquire from the residue of the dust. From the fragments of shattered dreams. An effort for you so that you will see the light while it shines. Not to have to navigate the space between, but to actually see what's on the page. An effort to show you what no one could reveal to me. It may not work—but it's an effort, after all.

But my wish for you is to make much more than an effort. My wish for you is to put in the greatest of efforts, with the absolute certainty that it will reach its destination. An effort in the right direction. The effort that leads everywhere—including directly to yourself. This is the beginning— and ending—of all journeys. My wish for you is to find out now what it took me the better part of a lifetime to uncover—and indeed, almost took a life in the process. Call this an exercise in effective time management (to put it in more practical terms, even though this is far from the point—but perhaps it will make more sense to you at this time). I had to lose everything in order to find it again. It is my hope to convey that journey to you in these pages.

You might say I'm attempting to open a lane for you if you happen to be stuck in traffic. I encourage a switch to the fast lane, as opposed to the carpool variety. Or, if you prefer, I'm your friendly neighbourhood car salesman, pitching you on the turbocharged upgrade.

The juice is worth the juice.

Life is my full-time gig. By that I mean it takes the maximum of my energy to participate in life on a functional level due to all the complications I will tell you about. Anything beyond that, such as this miracle in your hands, is currently gravy. It is my hope you use every moment that is not a struggle for existence as a struggle for excellence. What, for me, is gravy, shall be, for you, your meal—if you so desire. Do the opposite of what is expected. Don't go for comfort but for the struggle. My struggle has turned out to be showing up for life itself, so I encourage you to go far past me. And let me tell you: you can. Get to the stars, so I can hear the story. If you don't have a particular struggle, I would recommend that as yours.

There's no need to escape yourself, and even if there was, it's impossible. Believe me, I've taken every route there is, and they all lead back to the beginning. You won't get what you expect from this. Seriously, seriously. What will you get from this? To truly stand for something in this world, you must know you are not of it. You will get the uncut, not-made-for-TV version. I'll give you the way it was, the way it is, and the way it could be. You are your own support system.

Take a breath. Take another.

Are you getting it? Fear not—it only took me approximately forty years. What can I say? Somehow, I'm still here, able to tell the tale—so I figure I should.

Forward – Enter at Your Own Risk

This concerns you if you are concerned about you. This does not concern you if you are only concerned about the you that you knew. The you that does what you do. Only *you* can be concerned about you, because only you know what you do.

You are what's missing.

If I did it, you shall surely do far more.

Be better than what you know of yourself.

What you will get from me is the truth as it unfolded for me, without obligation or bias—at least as far as I can tell. What you will get from me is an honest attempt at contribution. To contribute nothing less than the psychic evolution of one willing participant.

I will ask you to take a leap into the ocean of possibility—the possibility you are more than you've ever dreamed. The possibility you are part of the grand design. That's not too much to ask, is it? What you will get from me is not what you may want to hear, nor what you may expect.

Consistently inconsistent, inconsistently consistent, inconsistently inconsistent, consistently consistent.

Predictably unpredictable.

Mind the gap, gap the mind, get in the gap, hit it in the gap, go to the Gap or maybe Old Navy or maybe the Army—make sure you warn me to keep the receipt—can you see it—did they seize it? Do you see it as fit? Did it fit? Find a size that fits then stay fit or stay fat or stay phat, make that putt, or stay put. Just say maybe and then maybe you may say something, or say nothing. Eat your peas, but please follow the recipe—oh, please, you didn't need to say please or sorry just for sneezing! What were you thinking? What is that stinking? Is it the stinking thinking, or is the ship sinking? What were they thinking? Stop thinking, start thinking—think about it! You've got to use your head—don't eat bread, grow dreads! Inhale, hail, don't inhale, go for a sale—quit drinking, start smoking—the smoking gun, where there's smoke there's fire—who started the fire? We didn't start the fire! There's fire—keep the fire burning—light it up, smoke 'em if you got 'em—but if you don't, you might hit the rock. The crack is where the light shines in—in through the out door—cover the crack but stay on track, cover the tracks in the summer, such a bummer. Don't bum her out—stay out late! What can you do other than what you do? What do you do? Do you do you? By the book. Buy the book. By the book. Buy the book. By the book. Buy the book. By the book.

Be all you already are. Be all you already were. Be what you are going to be.

Enter at your own risk, Own your risk, enter. Risk your own entrance. You're at risk of owning your entrance. Risk owning your entrance. Play more Risk. Enter your own risk. Risk at your own. You're now at risk of entrance. At risking, you own.

CHAPTER 1

Arrival

These were the days... or so I've been told. How do you tell a story you weren't really there for? That is the mystery of the beginning of this journey.

I suppose it will have to be about trust. I have to trust the majority of events I was told took place at St. Michael's Hospital after the event of June 4, 2010 actually happened, because I certainly wasn't "there." For the most part, physically, I was, but the rest is a blur. The only memory is leaving there on what I believe to be June 24, 2010. I was being transported to Lyndhurst Hospital in Toronto, which was where parts of this mystery started to come clear.

In the interim, I was told many things about my time at St. Michael's, and upon revision, most make some amount of sense. I was told of visitors—some I vaguely recall, while most are only an idea, though it makes sense they would have been there. The most significant aspect of this period was my medical situation, which again, I have had to re-examine, but which, with the passage of time, for the most part, makes sense. The most tangible point is that I had been the victim of a hit-and-run incident on June 4, 2010 in Toronto, after which I had been admitted to St. Michael's Hospital downtown—at what time, I am not sure. The incident occurred in the southwest part of the city, in an area called Parkdale, where I was living at the time.

I have absolutely no recollection of any of this. My last memory is heading down the final street home from downtown on a bicycle—apparently, a few minutes before the accident. As the rest of the story goes, I was left in the street for an undetermined amount of time before a taxi driver called an ambulance. I don't really know the specific medical details after that, other than I was in a coma or unconscious state for some amount of time—days. I also know I was left with a spinal injury and brain damage. What I don't know is what treatments I underwent when I was admitted. Apparently, there were lots of strong painkillers and many other medications used to stabilize me and prevent the need for surgery—I wasn't operated on, so they were successful as far as I understand.

There had been a great fear of full paralysis which I thankfully averted but, I was left with an incomplete spinal cord injury and some amount of brain injury, which I still don't completely comprehend. Now, I really don't recall some specific moments waking up but I do recall wondering what had happened. Beyond that, I have only flashes of events. These include various visits from friends and family, most of whom, to this day, I don't know how they found out I was there. For the ones I recall, it was only for a brief moment. To all who came, I am eternally grateful.

I do recall sleepless nights, which are standard for hospitalizations in my experience, but I couldn't tell you anything exact. Apparently, lawyers started showing up, which I recall even more vaguely—though again, it makes sense that they were there. There were flashes of the doctors and nurses, but nothing close to anything like what I have been told was reality: apparently it was an endless stream of medical professionals. It must be true, because my lack of clarity at that time seems to indicate being on a tremendous amount of very strong medication, which would also indicate the circumstances were quite dire.

The strangest aspect of that period of time is that I don't recall a particular mental state of any type. One would have expected some amount of pain, fear, or perhaps doubt. If that was the case, I have no memory of it. Perhaps I actually was asleep the entire fourteen days. It really is odd I cannot recall having any extreme reaction to having had a very serious accident that resulted in major and catastrophic injuries with definite, lifelong consequences. I really cannot account for this, as it makes no sense. It must be similar to the reason why I only have memory of a few minutes before the incident. Narcotics are known to cause this phenomena. Whatever the reason, that was and is the case. Perhaps I was blessed with ignorance of reality. It was simply a time of indifference, more or less. I have been told since that I was in some state of shock and I wasn't fully yet awake. I'm not certain exactly what that means, but again, it seems to make sense. But I have no idea how this has manifested itself—or better yet, exactly how and when I came out of that state.

This period of my existence is therefore but a concept. To this day, I cannot personally verify any of the supposed facts of that time with even one iota of certainty. What I can say was that I was on my way home on a bike, like a bat out of hell (which was by no means unusual) from a music gig downtown, back to Parkdale. That journey was a regular one then. All was well until the very moment it wasn't. My mind disposed of the memory of this transition. I have since been informed I was hit from behind by a rather large vehicle that immediately fled the scene as I lay motionless in the street. Why this happened and who did this to me has remained a mystery. There was nothing about my lifestyle at the time—which was more or less that of a dropout hippie—that would invite the creation of enemies. Then again, that is my assumption—who can really say? I can definitely say I was unaware of any incidents that would have given anyone the motivation to commit such an act.

I was rescued by the taxi driver who called the ambulance and police. I am about to resume a quest to locate this individual. If not for that divine intervention, I would most likely have faced a fate far worse. I have also been told that the relatively short passage of time between when I was hit and help arrived was a key factor in how things ultimately played out. I also seemed to have been protected by the Fender Stratocaster on my back that night. It appears to have absorbed enough of the impact to keep me in one piece. After seeing pictures of the incident and the size of the vehicle, I know that must have been the case. Perhaps that's really why this instrument has the reputation it does! Again, who can say for sure? But it seems to fit. That has turned out to be the obvious theme of this initial phase.

The other apparent major aspect of the St. Michael's chapter were the medical procedures that took place. I have been told I arrived unconscious in the early hours of the morning that day. I have also been told that the doctors were uncertain how to proceed due to the extremely sensitive nature of the injuries in the spine and brain. Uncertain about paralysis, they had to proceed cautiously. I have been told I was constantly being moved around the hospital due to rapidly shifting circumstances, in order to conduct various tests to find out exactly what had taken place. Again, all that was news to me.

After much apparent deliberation and time, the conclusion was made that partial paralysis had occurred, but surgery was not required. Instead, the chosen treatment was heavy steroids in conjunction with other medications, of which I am still uncertain. I don't know if I was in the most critical section of the hospital, but from how it was described, the situation was quite dire and uncertain at the time. Apparently, this was when the drug treatment for spinal swelling began, along with treatment for a fracture at the back of my head—of what I believe is known as the occipital bone. Again, this seems to add up. There was also kidney damage and other related injuries, which also became apparent there. I was told I was there for two to three days before being moved to a regular room. I don't know at what exact point that move was made, but I would assume I had attained a certain point of stability. It was around that time that other friends and family began visiting. I still wasn't moving or speaking much, my head was bandaged and my neck was being held straight with some device. It apparently took a week to even get my teeth cleaned. After a week, I still wasn't speaking, and by that time, I was on a morphine drip—which I'm assuming was for pain. After two weeks, I still wasn't fully conscious.

I was told that sometime during the second week I began to wake up or become more conscious. I still don't know what that exactly meant in practical terms, but perhaps I was more aware of what was happening. Again, I will have to take their word for it. At some point in the second week, legal discussions and implications also commenced. That could be another book in itself. There apparently was some concern I would not be able to sign my own documents within the required amount of time. However, my mother confirmed this did become possible. I cannot say what the complications would have been had this not been the case, but I'm certain it wouldn't have been too pleasant for anyone involved.

I can tell you that today, I am able to walk—which was admittedly in jeopardy for some time. I do not know what they did about my brain and all the damage, but I can tell you that it did happen. It remains miraculous to me that I recall precisely *none* of the procedures and the dates. My life was in the balance, and I was not there! What insanity! I can tell you precisely none of the day-to-day details of my approximate ten-day stay there. It may have been intensive care, though, so it may have been different in some ways from a typical hospital stay. I couldn't tell you. It is also mysterious that I can't recall even one other patient, nurse, doctor, or anyone in any other capacity from that time—and I am certain that there were many of them.

Many years after the fact, I've had it explained that the brain has some mechanism to protect itself after intensive trauma. I cannot explain this in more precise terms, but it seems to fit... or perhaps it was the cornucopia of medications. At some point, in the midst of all I've described, most likely after the most immediate and major threats were averted, discussions about my discharge must have begun. Perhaps I had demonstrated enough progress in some regard, because I can confirm I am no longer there. I have no idea how the ultimate decision was reached to transfer me to another hospital called Lyndhurst, a rehabilitation center in North Toronto that specializes in spinal cord injuries. This location was somewhat isolated compared to St. Michael's, and I suppose they had the most appropriate treatment for my injuries. Again, I can't give any specifics. But the decision was made, and I suppose preparation began immediately.

So this was how is was to be? The beginning of the unfolding mystery. Of course, it was news to me. The long and winding road to somewhere had begun. Where to stand? Could I stand? Could I stand it? What was the plan? Get up and run? Hit and run? A crime or part of the fun? Was it all done? What could I become? Was the work done, or had it just begun? The race was on, the time had come, the battle was won, but the war had just begun... time to move on, look to the beyond, the time had come, step one, step two, step three... all these questions to me, but what can they see? Did they know what was left of me, what was left to be, or just a matter of the fee? Seriously—it was news to me. First step on a journey no one knows—through the darkness, through the snows—and the rain, later comes the pain,—and struggle—get going on the double. Time to move? On and on, and on and on, and on and on, and on and on, and on and on. It goes.

I don't know how many days passed in this fashion before an official discharge date and plan was arrived upon. To my best current estimation, I was there for a total of ten days, so I would say the deliberations went on for the better part of a week. Again, who can really say how such a critical decision is arrived at? My best guess would be that the doctors got to a point at which they believed they had done what was required, or possible at that institution—or that the critical stage had passed. Whatever the case may have been, the ball was rolling.

It would have been good to know what the specific factors were in determining I had made enough progress to be deemed fit to move on to more rigorous rehabilitation and the wider "community." Was it physical, mental—a combination? Most likely, a combination—and other factors involved. I imagine everyone who showed up during that initial phase was also a part of this, because again, *I* surely wasn't. I would say, now, that the most critical factor was my partial paralysis diagnosis. A further explanation is that the clinical diagnosis was an incomplete spinal cord injury. This mostly affected the lower body. This must have meant, at the time, that with further, specialized rehabilitation, my ability to walk again, along with other functions, could be regained. Meanwhile, with a complete spinal cord injury, which involves a severing or breaking of the cord, it is generally not possible to regain such abilities, as I've come to understand. This, for me, was nothing short of a miracle, because this was a game of far less than inches, and if the point of impact had been even less than that of a split hair, this story would be infinitely different—or indeed, not possible at all. Over the years, I have met many who have faced a far different fate, though the initial circumstances were similar. One of the mysteries within this mystery is why I was spared.

I have absolutely zero recollection of any of these proceedings. The fact I was able to sign was another twist of fate that allowed this work to manifest. In the midst of all this, after taking in all factors mentioned here—and many others, I'm sure—the final collective decision was made to stay the course with the Lyndhurst plan. Again, it is far from the norm for a choice critical to one's fate to be made while one isn't actually "there." I don't know how many can say this, but it was the case for me. Again, I have no recollection of the scenario described, but it must have happened, because I'm telling the tale. At this juncture, I cannot find anymore items of significance from my time at St. Michael's. It was the maiden voyage on an expedition I will lay bare for you here. The projected returns on this investment are twofold. Mine—and more importantly, yours. The objective being for you to do far better than me—and better yet, far better than you've ever imagined.

I also got another recent report—this time, from a great friend who had visited me at St. Michael's and most other stops on the way up to this point. Their account is completely different, however. They claim I was in a very angry state, complaining about everything, including staff and food. Anger management issues are something that I recall manifesting much further down the road, and will probably be the topic of an entire chapter. They even went as far as to say they were sorry for the hospital staff, that they said I was somewhat "abusive" while they were there. This is a radical shift from my mother's account of my virtually unconscious state. It seems a bit impossible to be yelling at people if you aren't even able to speak, I don't know at what point, exactly, my friend visited, but it must have been closer to my discharge. It certainly seems odd to have the capacity for anger but no capacity to recall it. I suppose it depends on who you ask. I suppose that type of behaviour could have been possible, and perhaps even likely, but again, I have practically zero recollection of anything.

This brings up the idea of trust, an overriding theme of this initial phase, because I have very few precise memories of my own. This theme intensified as the journey progressed, and I have ultimately learned to be very selective in this regard. Trust is not something I give away blindly— if, in fact, I ever completely do anymore. The reasons for this are myriad, and I'm not saying this particular friend was violating my trust with their account. It is simply their current description of a situation from a quite distant past. It could be the passage of time has changed them to such a degree that this version of events now appears plausible. They have nothing to gain either way, but it does highlight this vital element of my story—and of course, the human condition. I, of course, can't argue either way. What I do know is that trust is something I pretty much keep for myself these days. This is as a result of my injuries themselves, most likely, but more tangibly, from an extended legal/insurance battle and various other incidents I will go into far more detail about later.

I have come to understand the majority of people are unpredictable, and, when the stakes are high, they may go in a different direction than they previously have. Be that as it may, this initial scenario—and many subsequent ones—put me in a position of *having* to trust, regardless. When in such a dilemma, all one can really do is put forth the best effort one is capable of and leave the rest up to fate. As a matter of fact, my current existence was made possible by that very notion.

I am certain there were many at St. Michael's who went far above and beyond the call of duty to keep me here. Perhaps the reason was to tell this story—or perhaps that's just what they do. Who can really say? I do know my time there laid the foundation for what was to come, and if I hadn't made it through, and then out of there, I wouldn't be here today.

CHAPTER 2

Awakening

"What's to happen now?", I most likely semi-consciously wondered as I was being transferred from inside a medical vehicle to Lyndhurst one early summer morning in June 2010. That was one of the more poignant moments of "waking up," as I distinctly recall being completely aware of what was taking place, while also being completely uncertain where things were headed. This state was probably in accordance with the decision to move me at that point. It is a fair distance from the downtown location of St. Michael's to the relatively uptown location of Lyndhurst. I do not recall anything coherent during that trip other than a bittersweet mix of curiosity and fear regarding my next step into the beyond. Little did I know my past had been radically preparing me for the ensuing chapter. Before this time, I had been living what most would term "a wanderer's existence." I may have preferred to have called it a wanderer's *path*, if you like. I was in search of wonder, as it was—of random adventure, on a quest for non-attachment and truth.

It is important to know Lyndhurst Spinal Cord Rehabilitation Hospital, part of Toronto Rehab, was at the time and most likely still is considered one of the best of its kind in Canada, and, as far as I know, the world. I know this because I met other patients there from all over the world. This is of note because in spite of this, some patients never recovered, some healed more than others, and some made minimal progress, even though they were there for the same amount of time and their injuries, at least to my untrained eye, appeared to be quite similar.

I mention this because, during my extended three-and-a-half-month stay, I witnessed many other patients come and go, and I observed their progress or lack thereof. Some improved rapidly, while many others didn't—and some, in fact, seemed to deteriorate. Granted, there could be endless factors I wasn't privy to—that's just how it appeared to my layperson's eyes.

Nevertheless, I noticed all the people who were successful had a radically different attitude to those who weren't. From what I could gather, they were able to stay in the moment as opposed to dwelling in the losses brought by their misfortune. The patients who were not as fortunate spent a significant portion of their days lamenting what seemed to be lost or gone. As far as I could tell, the first way allowed one the opportunity to take full advantage of the tremendous resources available, and thus make progress, while the other made significant—and critical—amounts of time pass, and regression to sometimes occur. I went on to discover the initial phases of recovery from spinal cord injury are vital to the possibility of long-term recovery and progress. Upon witnessing similar scenarios repeatedly and taking advantage of the resources available, I undertook an unofficial study of the philosophy of success, in order to really examine the possible role one's attitude or mentality might play in the attainment of goals throughout the course of history.

My path proceeded in many directions, over many years, with many routes, with accompanying guides, and ultimately led me to a place of emancipation from a self that no longer proved to be useful. It also led to a refusal of labels or titles, with the knowledge they were all futile and only served the purposes of a false ego. The methods practised were varied—some more disciplined, most riskier—none of which, probably, would be recommended to try at home! It all led to my goal to go further into the mystery and pass on the knowledge to those who have ears to hear it. That was the deal—in a nutshell, anyway. You might say the mission was to keep on keeping on in order to awaken others—with the ultimate vision of global celebration, essentially. Prior to my accident, I had yet to experience any tragedy so major it could drastically alter one's direction. There had been drama and various misfortunes that had led me to the search for truth in the first place, but nothing that had had such a physically altering—and thus even *more* life-altering element.

Part of my unofficial education up to that point had been much study of non-Western philosophies. I had found it all ultimately led to a shedding of layers of material illusion to get to a place of presence, thus removing doubt and fear in order to function in authentic reality. Of course, there were various titles for these varied paths—but this seemed to be their common goal. They also had more subtle elements surrounding faith, destiny and karma, among other things. However, they all converged on the same point. I had found a vital concept in all of this, which was to be able to play different roles when necessary—and, in so doing, not be attached to any, so that when one reaches one's end, as we all surely will, there isn't a problem. One simply moves on to the next role, as an actor in a play might do. I was about to discover just how vital a concept that was.

I began to discover that, invariably, one's focus and state of mind is the most critical factor. In fact, it turned out to be far more valuable than any external or material element could ever be. It seemed to be the *only* tool one actually needed to achieve one's objective. Being injured and in hospital, some may believe medications, doctors, the severity of one's injury, one's tools and technology, and so on may be the ultimate determinants, but I began to find evidence to the contrary—accounts that one could literally heal themselves from the inside. These theories had a lot to do with the concept that one's attitude and focus could—or, in fact, routinely *would*—be the vital determinant in achieving a desired result. In this case, the desired result would be a successful recovery from spinal cord injury—specifically in *my* case, this would be regaining the ability to walk—which, at the beginning of Lyndhurst, was no certainty.

Essentially, if you can see it, you can achieve it. This is putting it far too simply, but for the purposes of this work, it applies. What I can tell you without a shadow of a doubt is that every patient I observed at length that was not able to get into the present moment of their circumstances—and create a tangible goal and work toward it—did not fare well. As stated, those that chose the opposite, achieved the opposite.

Some of these examples were roommates of mine, so I observed them on a regular and continuous basis. Seeing this as clear evidence of a theory, I proceeded with the latter option.

Basically, my full-time job was to strengthen my body as much as possible in order to facilitate its ability to walk after sustaining spinal damage in the lower region and at least a few weeks of immobility. There was also the matter of some amount of brain injury—but that is definitely another story. So, every day, bright and early, like a normal human, it was off to the specialized gym to find out what new experiment the physio had come up with—and to go through it over and over, all day and week, or longer, until it got the intended result.

Sometimes would be more painful than others, but I would always complete the task, no matter what. That's the thing with a situation like this: there is no waiting for tomorrow, because tomorrow almost didn't happen. The ability to participate in life with any degree of effectiveness was hanging in the balance, and the nature of this injury is that regression happens much more rapidly than progress—and I was determined *not* to be in the hospital permanently.

With this knowledge, the mission was clear: get it done. This mostly meant everything involved in getting walking—which was a lot. It also meant proceeding through many sleepless nights, visiting a psychologist almost daily, practising guitar during the times when the gym wasn't possible, refusing friends' offers of "medicine," asking for as many extensions as possible at Lyndhurst, along with figuring out housing after discharge—basically, always having an eye on the finish line. It's important to note what a radical shift this was from my previous existence.

I had a life that, now, is difficult to describe, due to the passage of time. In fact, it seems to be another life altogether. Ironically, being difficult to categorize was by design—some might say it was just being difficult. My purpose up to then—specifically while I was in Toronto—had been to live in such a way as to expose the illusions in what we call society here in North America. The other goal was to find the truth, apart from what most were taught to believe. I believe I was successful at this—though not in the typical sense. But that was the point. It had been a somewhat nomadic existence, but somehow, through that, I found my tribe.

That was the miracle of it: finding the island in the urban jungle. My life had been a journey of miracles, in fact, and at some point, I had to discover that indeed, *everything* was, if you had the eyes to see it. To me, it was perplexing why everyone couldn't see it—especially when in a place of such material abundance. Yet, it was apparently easier to keep one's eyes closed and stumble along. I found out, at some point, that it was drastically more important to learn to let go than to acquire or possess. It seems counterintuitive in a materialistic society, but I got endless results from it. The miracle of it is that I was able to maintain a reasonable existence in these circumstances while practising absolutely none of this society's norms. Some may call this questionable, but I found the entire system questionable—and that judgement, I suppose, is good for them but didn't move me one way or the other. My judge isn't on this plane. My mission was to spread these messages in whatever form possible while maintaining myself.

The extensions were over; I was fine with the current commune, but the lease was up. However, I don't recall there being a tremendous amount of trepidation or fear arising in the days preceding my departure. Perhaps this was due to the knowledge that I would return to Lyndhurst regularly as an outpatient, in combination with the training I had been giving myself, on the benefits of trust and faith. Or maybe it was all that, and in addition, having the knowledge of where I had come from, and that there was no way I was going back to that. What I do know is that fear automatically makes everything worse, so, the elimination of it increases the odds immensely, in any situation.

Fear, what more can be said about fear? I have come to find that it is most often, only an illusion, with no basis in reality. For example, previous to this, I would have said that spending extended time, essentially living in a hospital, would be, a terrible thing, but it turned out to be quite the opposite. In my previous existence, I had also found this concept to be true, when having to start over, change status, identity etc., on many occasions. Now, I have come to say, go further into the unknown: the truth, your truth is there. It isn't to be found in the safety of comfort or familiarity. Neither will you see it in attachment. I can only say these things because I was forced away from all these and more, even the unconscious reliability of my own body, in rapid fashion, and found that something far greater remained. You don't know what you don't know. So, proceed.

So, there I was once more, heading into another reality: this time, the Bellwoods chapter. That was the name of the place I was headed to next.

CHAPTER 3

Stepping Up

On one particularly usual day, early on in my stay at Bellwoods, when it was still quite uncertain how the next immediate phase was going to unfold, as no secure housing had been found, I headed out on a sojourn in search of the past. This meant taking a "walk" to Kensington Market, which was now, literally, just down the street. As I was still using a walker at the time, even this distance could often be a great challenge. Upon heading out, I noticed that there was a significant amount of construction, directly impeding my path to the destination, for quite a distance. Upon more detailed observation, I also noticed that there was a small path, immediately in front of me, also leading to the intended destination. I took this as a profound sign to just keep taking the next step, and the road would be created. So I did. So did I. On the surface, you may not notice the profundity of this event, but I certainly did. It represented continued hope and possibility. If I could make it back to Kensington regularly, that meant a chance to recreate my authentic life, as far as I was concerned at that time. It also meant that there were greater forces still at work, that had solutions where I saw literal roadblocks. This was a significant moment which allowed progress to continue.

Another key aspect of my time at Bellwoods was my interaction with fellow clients. I prefer to call this fellowship. This was indeed bittersweet, sweet for the unique understanding to be found amongst such a community, of those who could really "get it". On the bitter side, was the continued realization that this type of setting, or similar ones, would have to play a major role in whatever life was to bring.

This setting was also the stage at which more extended debate of my legal situation commenced. What do I mean by this? Well, the debates went from possibilities to realities. The specifics of dates numbers began to come into ever sharper focus. I was initially quoted a period of two years, to get from the present point to the settlement. That seemed reasonable then. I went ahead. At the same time, there began discussion of the strategy that would take place on my end, and perhaps more critically, on the other, or, "their" end, as it were. I use the confrontational tone now, as it did turn into a battle, but at the time, things were still cordial, on all sides. I should let you know that the nature of the legal beast is to be at war, which I was to discover in due, or, more precisely, undue time. So we were in the initial stages of the deliberations on my case. All this procedure was news to me, as my only previous experience with the law, had been going to any lengths, not to be involved in it, on any level. As mentioned, my goal had been to find the timeless laws—now I was to be bound by the man-made variety, for an indeterminate amount of time, despite a reasonable estimate of two years having been given.

There was debate about the specific methods that the other side might be employing. I was told that one of them could've been observing my daily life and movements, in order to possibly make the claim that I was "faking it", essentially. I had heard of this sort of thing before, or seen it in movies, perhaps, but it was still somewhat surprising. Ponder the depths of it for a moment: someone has their entire reality drastically altered, then has to potentially hide like a criminal? It wasn't exactly as cut and dried as that, but you get the point. My lawyer explained to me that pain and suffering had to be tangible and real. As far as I was concerned, it already was. At that point I was getting prepared for the scenario of having to prove something that someone else had done. Essentially, I was also learning how to hide in plain sight, meaning that I had to prove my inability to perform tasks which used to be routine. This would ultimately morph into obvious and blatant undercover observation of me— being spied upon. This all added to the notion of heading into worlds and realms, which I had no knowledge of or any desire to sign up for. Once again, however, the only option was to keep going.

There was also discussion of numbers, which might potentially be realized at the end of the road. These sounded somewhat reasonable, but definitely not stupendous. There was also explanation of how the process in the interim was to be. Specifically, what would most likely take place on a day-to-day basis, between now and then. There was also talk about the conditions which might be put on me, in order to receive the benefits at the end. So, the plan was to stay the course of whatever stipulations the insurance company might conjure up. It was either that or go back to the start. Too late for that. This was roughly the scope of legal matters at the time, before they began to take on a life of their own.

At this point, outpatient physiotherapy continued on the same scale, more or less. Probably about 3-4 days a week, after travelling approximately 30 minutes, depending on traffic, from downtown to uptown. The reason I mention the commute, is that the mode of transportation at that point, was a service called Wheeltrans. This service is designed specifically for those with disabilities, of such a nature, that typical modes of transportation do not suffice. This took the form of either a car, or a much larger, utility type of vehicle. When it was the latter variety, it was deemed necessary to strap me in, I would say, rather excessively. This was apparently for my own safety, but it appeared to me more as torture, or prison. Compared to how I used to travel on the wind, this was cumbersome, but apparently necessary. Necessary for whom, I often wondered? Yet another mystery to accept, I suppose. When one has this manner of injuries, one's choices become altered. At this point, I wouldn't say altered for the worse, but they become, perhaps, more limited and calculated; priority becomes the order of the day, as maintenance of these ailments is essential given there is no "cure". There is no pill for brain and spinal injuries, at least not to my current knowledge. The real medication and treatment is routine, structure and regular crisis management! Simply put, you're in for the long haul, there's no short cut through this one. There has to be more planning and time to get previously routine matters done, and nothing, I repeat, nothing can be taken for granted. For me, all of this was quite novel; previously, my only real concern was to find some way to afford whatever I was up to, at whatever particular time.

The days at Bellwoods went by in much the manner I have described. The most pressing issue was housing. Such a shame that material aspects are always put ahead of all the rest, especially in the case of those who don't have much choice at all, or had some other misfortune, through no fault of their own. Such was my case at the time. This is what the world has backwards: so it was; so it is. I was only going to be there for six months, the reason being that the injuries weren't severe enough to warrant a longer, or permanent stay. Or, perhaps enough progress had been made to enable whoever makes these decisions, to determine that a long-term stay at Bellwoods, wouldn't be necessary. It would seem to make sense to me, to keep someone in a situation that has had good results, for as long as possible, but these things have never made sense, and this book is about finding your own sense through the non-sense. Regardless, since I no longer lived in Parkdale, I was now on a waiting list for Toronto Housing. This was a process I had been through many, many years before, and I back then, it took far longer than six months to find my own apartment—this time, there were the added requirements of accessibility and a downtown location.

Material abundance would be another new adventure. I hadn't experienced much of this side of life since childhood, when one is blissfully unaware of what one possesses as being different from what one may not, as it is all one has ever known. This need for money, and the reality that it was the only form of justice available to me, at the time, were the chief justifications in my going forward with the legal process. At that point, I was unaware of the benefits, or dangers that increased financial resources could bring, so, in that sense, I thought of it as returning to a childlike state.

The gift of vanity is only more of the same, so who you gonna blame, when you get trapped in the game?

I once heard someone say, don't ask, why me? Ask, why not me? Please do this constantly in conflicted times.

Through all these new forks in the road, my eyes were still on the finish line. The focus for that goal, continued to be the new physiotherapy routine, which was now in addition to the more limited outpatient program at Lyndhurst. I'm not exactly certain how many days a week I was going there, but I am certain that it was the maximum all involved would, or could, allow. These occasions were an opportunity to take all the negative energy from the various games being played and put it into the higher purpose of rising above it all, and creating a future.

What I'm saying is that this was another unexpected hurdle to climb. I had the assumption that being in Canada the types of discriminations/ policies I was beginning to experience didn't exist. The lack of complete accessibility at that time, though worse then but still existent today, proved otherwise. I'm not saying it's not better than other countries, but what's the point of comparing to a negative? This is where we live and the reality we exist in. Anything else is a fantasy and my entire point in this book is to get out of fantasy. Canada also professes the fantasy of equality in all areas and I have definitely found that this is not case where disability is considered. Find your own truth in all cases both inner and outer. Don't blindly accept what's handed out to you. I'm saying this because I would have believed that those with "disabilities" and more extreme circumstances would be treated better than the mass of the population but the opposite proved to be the case a significant amount of the time.

Typically it takes years to get a private, subsidized apartment in the Toronto Housing system. I know because I had already been through that and had paid my dues to get the 1 bedroom unit that I did have. People don't typically give those up because of the fear of not getting back in. Due to a lack of accessibility there was no choice in my case as explained previously. I can't recall what the other possibilities were but a bachelor unit not far away on Bloor St. became an option. I don't know how much of a "choice" it really was nor how much of a real option a tiny apartment in a building with a notorious drug history really was either, but so it was. I believe the other places with availability had even more issues and what can I say, you take what you can get when in such a dilemma. It wasn't a done deal, however, I remember there being various issues with the current tenant in regards to them moving. This merry/ go-round ride went on for some time. I can't recall what the specific issues were, perhaps something surrounding mental health/addiction which were common amongst people needing housing. I can say so because I was one and have had those issues, among others. I don't see that particular living situation as a loss however. The majority of people in this city, especially currently, live in dwellings much smaller or with roommates of various numbers with a horrific daily commute to job they need to do to continue to afford it. The only real difference is that you're not fully in control of your own destiny. When you rely on someone else for anything you are also subject in equal amount to their desires. In subsidized housing, you cannot do as you wish in your residence, you must follow their rules which you may not agree with and may end up questioning whose benefit they are actually in.

Subsidized housing does provide physical shelter but that's about where it ends. Unfortunately, that's of life's least value as I've come to find out. Don't get me wrong, I'm not biting the hand that fed. There was a time when it was required and I am grateful for that and it is a tragedy that the general cost of living is absurd. What I am saying is don't seek convenience and the illusion of comfort; you will not find much there other than stagnation. Never seek the low-hanging fruit, go for the top of the tree. It's a harder climb but that's where the light is. Go for the sky and you'll probably get the moon as they say. Never limit yourself, you are from an endless place and charity is limited. If you follow another's vision you make yourself blind. But you are the seer. Give away what you don't require and the truth is that you already have all you need and more. Seek the narrow path at all times, the reward will be your own. What does all this have to do with waiting to get an apartment at Bloor/ St.George in downtown Toronto? Well, it was the best I could do at the time. It was presenting itself as the next logical option, the next thing rising from the ashes. This is what I would ask you to do, always seek the best for yourself, whatever requires your utmost in all areas. Leave the rest for the crowd. The crowd is for you! Not the other way around.

The days carried on much like this, waiting for word on the Bloor St. possibility while being involved in the other activities. The problem is, the longer you stay somewhere the more attachments develop. That was definitely the case there. As more time went by I got to know everyone better and spent more time in those evening gatherings and during the day at Lyndhurst and occasionally I would now run into the same people in various parts of town. I would also start to ponder what an ideal location and apartment it was and that only god knows what the market rent would be. But, as I said, the only thing free in this world is one's own effort along with what was put here before any of us arrived. Nonetheless, this is what happens and I was in no man's land as it were, waiting in limbo, which is a dangerous place. This illustrates my previous point of controlling your own fate. The only reason the process was taking this long was the nature of the arrangement. This was perhaps part of the riddle of life it itself. How to go through it all without becoming damaged or perhaps a victim. My answer is to know how to be in the crowd and by yourself, sometimes at the same time but that's another book. It starts by knowing how to be by yourself without being forced into it. Alone but not lonely.

I was quite sick of it all at this point and I believe the six months had passed. You get what you pay for I suppose, and when the price in dollars is virtually 0, I've come to learn that you can expect virtually anything. So, here I was once again in an enforced limbo, this time, not at my own request.

Close to this time I was beginning to get a clearer picture of the legal situation that I now had become involved in. It turned out to be a hit and run incident in the very early morning. They ended up getting caught in a version of "Canada's Dumbest Criminals." when returning the rental car as best I can recall. It remains a mystery to me why someone did this as I was never involved in any type of circle that would condone such an act. Their argument, of course, was that it was unintentional or somehow my fault, which was completely ludicrous. I believe there were several meetings with my lawyer at the time surrounding this issue, in his effort to be certain that I had absolutely no role in it. It's a strange reality having to attest to your own innocence when it's blatantly obvious to anyone with a brain what actually happened. I have also come to find out that the legal game is not one where logic is a key player. We were beginning to get into the specifics of a potential settlement and what that would involve and how it was that I might be eligible for one in the first place. This had to with the fact that the vehicle that struck me was rented, meaning that there was an insurance company, which meant that there were funds available for such incidents and compensation for such incidents. The issue then became convincing this company that I was actually the victim and of what was then a reasonable amount. This is a bit of a bizarre concept because as far as I know, the other party didn't end up in hospital or have their life forever altered by a vicious act not of their own choosing.

My lawyer began to break down the specific details of all this and how exactly this compensation would be calculated and the various factors in the case and how it would possibly all unfold in the most likely scenario. A long-term settlement is based off a number generated from a reasonable expectation of lifetime losses and in the short-term there was something called a "non-earner benefit" for increased costs of living. I also found out that one becomes eligible for such things if one's injuries are deemed to be "catastrophic" by the appropriate doctor. I don't know that fortunately is the right word for such a thing but I was categorized as exactly that at some point before leaving Lyndhurst. The lawyer was quite glad about that turn of events because if you're not, then your chances of any reasonable compensation are apparently slim to none. In light of the options this could be seen as a positive because the fact again was that there was no going back and life was going to cost more in very real terms. All of this was the the tip of the iceberg in my unofficial legal education in the realm of motor vehicle accidents and all that encapsulates. In my previous incarnation, I did all I could to distance myself from "the law", now it seems I was in bed with them. Once again, it seemed to fit. I was still running on faith in all crucial matters and this was to be another and perhaps the most critical. I knew nothing of this lawyer. He came on my mother's recommendation and that was all I had to go on. So there it was, I signed up for yet another journey to parts unknown.

Some days later, the call came in that the apartment was ready. There was no time for hesitation as I was already past the mandated time at Bellwoods. So, bags were packed, I's dotted, T's crossed, goodbyes said and luck wished to the comrades. On to the next episode, another day in the life, another chapter over.

CHAPTER 4

Downhill

So, off it was to 341 Bloor St. West to a bachelor subsidized apartment. It was almost literally down the street from Bellwoods but once again may as well have been a world away in terms of changes that would happen to my daily reality. This building was in what most would call the downtown core in an area called The Annex, quite desirable by most standards. For me, again, it wasn't really a matter of choice, it was what was available and the next step on the path.

I still don't know how sensible it was to live in such a small space while having mobility issues, but so it was. This was seen by all involved as the next step towards independence, I don't know that a physical location has much to do with that but the levels of assistance were also significantly reduced here. There were no more live-in staff available in the building should any problems arise and there was also no one available to be contacted 24 hours a day for assistance with any matters. This was now only possible during regular business hours. There was, however, a team put together by my lawyer at the time to continue with the necessary aspects of continued progress and recovery. This consisted of a case manager, an occupational therapist and what I believe was titled, a rehabilitation support worker. Their roles, to varying degrees, were to assist in physical therapy in many forms, most notably, swimming at the time, relearning or learning new skills to do with vocation or daily life in general, navigating and transportation to an ever-increasing amount of legal and medical appointments, generally maintaining some sort of reasonable schedule and keeping things moving forward. I don't know if that much of it was actually needed but this is what was recommended at the time. I also began to find out that part of the game that goes on between the legal and insurance teams is that until there is a settlement, the former must continue to show and prove to the latter how much service their client does and will forever require even when this isn't exactly the case. This can be a slippery slope indeed.

These games are dangerous when you're not the one calling the shots. In some ways, you could say I was "calling the shots" in that all these people were only around because I was "choosing" to go forth with a legal case so there were resources to afford their services. On paper it may say so and it may also say that I was in charge of what they did or didn't do but is a choice really a choice when the other option is tantamount to giving up a chance at justice and the only real chance to improve a future already limited and altered due to the actions of another? I also wasn't made fully aware of the rules of this particular match before it started, nor did I have any knowledge of what the strategy of the opponent would be. So, you can see there really was no choice at all, nor was it a fair fight.

I am delving into this because it was around the time of taking up residence at Bloor St. that I began to be informed that I was more than likely being watched by the insurance company regularly to see what I was actually capable of on a daily basis so they could decide what they would pay for and what they would refuse and, probably most significantly, what they would have to pay for down the road. I can't say for certain that there were people watching me but I can tell that they did challenge a lot of requests for coverage in the areas of physical and mental rehabilitation which were obviously basic and necessary to me. Why else would I be going to so many doctors in town almost everyday if I didn't have to? I was also not so subtlety advised on more than one occasion to limit my activities and movements or in their words, "Don't push too hard." You can easily see the conflict of interests here. Up to this point, I had been doing exactly and nothing but that—pushing myself to the absolute limit in all regards to take full advantage of the life I had been spared and the opportunities that remained. Now I was supposed to voluntarily take my foot off the gas while still keeping an eye on the finish line. You can see the foul play here. But what can I say, I was already in or had "skin in the game."

So thus began a new way of living, of doing whatever I was doing but not really doing it, postponing activities I would normally do and at times literally hiding. Of course, all of this was happening while I hadn't done anything criminal but still had to act like some sort of fugitive. You can see the issues this could create and it certainly did. It had never been my way to play with smoke and mirrors, to create illusion, it was always to get free of the illusion. The only saving grace was that there was a far bigger goal in mind and this drama was not of my creation and this was the only road to justice. My eye was still on the finish line though it was now a bit more of a scenic route. To that end, I continued on with the various therapies at the time including swimming, continued outpatient programs at Lyndhurst, continued writing of articles for Outspoken magazine through Spinal Cord Injury Ontario, getting back into practicing music and general continued attempts at social reintegration and life reinvention. There was also the business of getting to know my new surroundings and locale, which was simple enough, having lived in Toronto for such a long time.

The new apartment building itself and its inhabitants were another story all together. Being half-subsidized, and, I believe, half market-cost, there was quite a unique combination of tenants. One group tended to be what appeared to be students from the nearby University of Toronto, or those who had chosen to live there for other reasons—most likely due to its proximity to the Annex and Yorkville, Toronto's downsized version of Beverly Hills. This group posed no issues, but the other group was another nation.

Having lived in a fully subsidized building before, I had an idea of what came with the territory—namely, the typical issues associated with lack of employment and resources. Though I was personally familiar with these, this place took them to another level. It must be noted that this building had been notorious for its history in the sixties, during which the area had been a haven for the flower child generation. I've been told that that location in particular was noted for its gatherings and associated vices and pleasures. I've been told these escalated through the years—which is no surprise, considering what I encountered there.

The name of it in the sixties was Rochdale, if memory serves—and if you care to investigate further. What I found among this particular population was more toward the dark side in terms of their lifestyles, as far as I could tell. There were many questionable characters and shady late-night scenes I observed out front on Bloor Street as the city passed by on its endless quest for what I'm not particularly sure. For those who don't know, Bloor is one of Toronto's most busy and popular streets, and a constant hive of activity, both day and night. I would observe the various characters, and of particular note were the apparently more unfortunate souls who would congregate very close to the building. There was obvious homelessness and drug trafficking and use by people I would regularly see in the building. I assumed they were tenants and noticed this activity daily. This was an issue for me.

I highlight this because I was on the path upward at this point, and this type of thing wasn't in my plans. Fortunately, I was still in the mode of putting all plans aside and proceeding with what was—but this element was certainly an unfortunate distraction (or roadblock, depending upon how you look at it). What I can say now is, be careful where you point the finger and who and what you judge.

On another front, there was the issue of the apartment itself. This turned out to be a real problem. I had applied for a unit similar to my previous one-bedroom, but all that surfaced in the required time was this bachelor. I had never before experienced a dwelling in which everything was one room, other than those long-gone days of forest-tent living when I had a body, mind, and soul that were, for the most part, untouched by extreme trauma or shock. Nevertheless, it was what it was, and I was promised I was on a waiting list for something more suitable and would be informed as soon as it was available. I was also told that I was given priority due to my medical condition. I have since learned to be leery of what most *say*, and only to pay attention to what gets *done*. But so it was—and time had to go on. I must also mention that a large part of the reason no one-bedrooms were available for me was the necessity that mine be accessible. There are far more regular units available. This is another travesty of the system we exist in: those who require more are most often subject to less. It was a mission in itself to fit all my worldly possessions into this space. Eventually, this was done, with the assistance of many, as I still had more physical capability to recover. So, here we were once again. This was the scene for my next reality.

By this point, I suppose, you could say I was reintegrating into the outside world in a reasonable fashion. Most people I knew were now aware of what had happened, and I was having more contact with them, since I was centrally located. The most significant adjustment was to the constant presence of various support workers on a routine basis. Prior to this, I was not one for rules or orders from anyone, and my own space and time were vital and necessary. That was not really an option at this point due to my full schedule of activities and the busyness of the location—and my urban version of a tent didn't help matters either.

So, what were the positives? Well, there were—and always are—many, but I first must give an accurate picture of what was taking place and what had to be overcome. The location was great in that it provided easy access to familiar surroundings, such as Kensington Market, even though things weren't quite the same. All the necessities of existence were close at hand, so this particular location would generally come at a premium, and I had heard that people typically wait up to ten years to find a spot at a reduced cost.

My main act of rebellion and progress at this point was to dispose of the walker that had been prescribed to me upon leaving Lyndhurst and continued to be recommended by most medical people involved in my case. To me, it represented all that had happened and all I planned to put behind me in rapid fashion, and since it wasn't absolutely necessary, I passed it on to Lyndhurst, for the sake of someone who could make more use of it. The medical establishment always deals in worst-case scenarios, but I have found that if that is what one fears, it tends to happen—and the opposite, I have also found to be true.

I was still practising my own methods of healing along with the traditional ones—and part of that was realizing the future can't happen if you stay in the past. It is also necessary to take risks to experience progress and growth. Now, having a walker, though it may have made things more comfortable and perhaps safe, to me, wasn't an advantage in the long run. I had learned a long time ago that safety and convenience do not lead to mastery and freedom, but more or less complacency and stagnation. On the surface, giving up the walker may seem like a simple choice, but as far as I know, when you get to a destination, you get rid of the map, and when summer is there, you take off the socks. What I'm saying is: use things only as far as they're necessary—or they end up using you! This was not part of my vision of crossing the finish line. So it was; so it is.

I told you I once heard someone say, "Don't ask why you—ask why *not* you." Again, please use this in times of tribulation and uncertainty.

Through all these new forks in the road my eyes were still on that finish line... It was no longer a straight line to get there, but so be it. My focus at that time became my new physiotherapy routine, which was in addition to the more limited outpatient program at Lyndhurst. I was now going to a place called Balance Physiotherapy. I'm not certain how many times a week, but I am sure it was whatever their maximum was given that insurance would cover. That was also the case at Lyndhurst. These became the locations where I put all the negativity from the games being played around me toward *my* endgame. Regardless of what others might or might not do, I was going to be around for no matter what happened (other than death itself). This was my higher calling, and wasn't between me and any other human but me and creation itself. This should also be your perspective when it comes to matters of priority.

The physiotherapy began with all sorts of assessments, which ultimately turned into something to get totally lost and disappear in, some type of refuge from the matters of the world. There were debates about the walker, but ultimately, they gave in, and the results were excellent. As a matter of fact, I maintain a relationship with my physiotherapy team to this day. This, again, was miraculous, because previous to all this, I could count on one hand the number of times I went to a gym. Try to find something where all the world disappears, and you appear.

One advanced version of the games being played were insurance agents' assessments of me. I suppose in some universe, these types of intrusions are justified, but not mine. They would come and test my abilities, even though they already knew damn well of my condition, because they were the very ones paying for my treatments. There had to be endless amounts of proof for these treatments to be approved in the first place. Believe me—insurance doesn't give money for nothing, and there is a price to pay. The facts were there—there's no faking a spinal cord injury. A brain injury, perhaps, but that would make you even crazier in the process.

So, what was really going on? Well, some of it might have been reasonable, or it might just be the nature of the beast. There did appear to be humans involved in it. Maybe there was some good and some of it was just the job. I believe they were trying to catch me in some sort of lie, to prove I was on a quest to get more money. Their entire goal is to give people nothing—or far less than they deserve.

What time did I have for such riddles? I was busy trying to use a life that had been spared, and time away from that to participate in some bureaucratic nonsense only served to create anger. I'm not certain how long this went on, but it was too damn long. These sessions became something to simply survive through. Ultimately, I did, but they served to feed the notion I had to defend myself, to prove my innocence, though I was the one with the injuries. These coincided with the mention of the strong possibility I was being watched by them, and on a few occasions, I did notice strange people in strange locations for long periods of time.

This was all becoming an issue as time passed, and it was making me reluctant to carry out my routines in a straightforward pattern. You can imagine the effect having the burden of proof on you when you're just building your reality. I'm not saying this was all bad. They did pay for lots of things, though most were a battle. I was granted a monthly benefit to supplement my disability payments for increased costs, and I was afforded what some might call luxuries, such as comfortable forms of private transportation to all appointments deemed therapeutic. All of this was beneficial, and perhaps I was fortunate, but none of it equaled the sense of my loss of freedom being trapped, which was increasing.

A prime example of the illogical and inefficient process at work was the fact that though a lot of treatments and activities were covered, they refused to pay for better accommodations. For what reason, I don't know. What they covered monthly far exceeded what it would have cost to do that, and I had doctor's letters saying where I was wasn't suitable. If the ultimate goal—as all parties professed it to be—was my speedy and long-term progress, a place with more space would have fit the bill perfectly.

What I'm saying to you is, don't play smoke and mirrors with anyone, especially yourself, and go all the way with whatever you do. Never be two-faced—that way, you can always live with yourself. That's how I've gotten through. If you're going to give, give it all with no conditions. Either do or don't—there's no in-between. You will only ever have one face, your original face, *the* original face—no masks necessary. This is your birthright: to simply be yourself. Anything else turns you into a commodity and any relationship into a contract. If you live in truth, there's no need to ever sign anything. I found that out by signing my life away hundreds of times. Yet I'm still here. Contracts are good for those who are planning to lie.

Now, my vision had become to get to the finish line with my soul intact. My body was coming along nicely, but it was becoming clear this was now a spiritual war—a fight to hold onto the best of me while creating the rest of me. What was real from the past was fading in the smoke and mirrors, but I still knew it was there—something that couldn't be taken away or bargained for. The highest hurdle to climb before the finish line was getting to the settlement. Without that, the race could not end. The timing was still uncertain—one year, two years, five years? No one seemed to know. I believe someone did, but this was still the world of liability, so no one was straightforward. I'm not saying there wasn't anyone on my side who could make a difference—there actually were many, and they did great things, but the nature of this beast was to walk a twisted road. I planned to cross that line, fully ready for the next life to begin, once I was free of these shackles. In the meantime, daily life had to continue.

The best one can ever hope is to solve an issue in a manner that lessens the burden of the issue; instead the solution I was offered was serving to increase that burden. This was my pseudo version of karma. When I unknowingly signed my freedom away for an uncertain length of time in order to solve the imminent financial issue I faced, I was risking losing everything else that mattered in the process. At the time, I didn't have this knowledge, but I still didn't have any choice but to press on. A dark cloud was building, though, with each interrogation and mention of surveillance or what my schedule was going to be and with whom. Perhaps this would have been tolerable for normal individuals, but I saw myself as far from that. I had done what was required to emancipate myself from the crowd, and now, due to the circumstances, I had gone completely the other way, and was now trapped amongst them for a crime I didn't commit. The cloud was going to burst.

Those trips to appointments in all manner of exceedingly comfortable private vehicles were the only times during that period I can recall getting away from my reality and rediscovering my true self, for the ever so briefest of moments. These were the moments when I would do something that had absolutely nothing to do with what I was supposed to be doing. I would go into some form of meditation to ask for the future to arrive, or to separate myself from the circumstances at hand. Those were one of the few times during that period, that I can recall really getting away from my reality. I took this respite to visualize the future, and to ask for whatever resources were required to get there. Basically, I took a timeout from the games.

Another thing I learned: the road is made by walking. I'm not certain if this wording is mine—I'm quite sure it isn't, actually, but it stumbled into my path at some point. So, if you're stuck, just keep going in any way possible. The path will present itself soon enough. There's a clearing just up ahead, just past where you can't imagine making it, just past where you can't see. Just one breath past what you imagine you don't have—your lungs are stronger, and you haven't even begun to use them yet. Just one more step.

At the time, I was in a race against time—which one never wins, of course. The days went on as days go on: more physio sessions, more interrogations, more possibilities of being under surveillance and all the rest of it. But as I was going on, I was gaining more knowledge and resilience and endurance. Some sense of possibility was also being gained; life was happening at the same time as the destruction, or rather the attempted destruction, of myself and my confidence in the truth, as I and everyone who knew me knew it, continued.

You see, there's a part of you no one can touch. You only find it in the darkness. So, try as they might, I wasn't participating in the games. Fortunately, I had knowledge of the untouchable place. This was something like being searched when you know you don't have anything, but they are convinced that you must. I have also experienced that. This is the world attempting to make you believe its story, to join the plot. But you're the star in this movie—so find out your story. My story was to continue with what I knew to be real, getting stronger, connecting with people and carrying out all the necessary routines as they were.

A few months or so had now passed, my walker was a distant memory, and my days of hospitalization were becoming one, too—even though I wasn't convinced this was necessarily better. For better or worse, life goes on. I was using a cane now, but I had visions of being free of that soon, too. In addition to the regular physiotherapy, there was now also regular hydrotherapy, which produced even more positive results. I saw no reason I had to be accompanied to those, but so it was. I believe acupuncture and massage therapy were introduced somewhere around then, too. Typically, these sorts of activities are seen as a form of leisure, but they were my work or duty. I attended them all religiously. I took as many sessions as the insurance would pay for—which was a quite a few, I must say. Again, it wasn't all bad—but the heart of it wasn't pure.

Sometime around then, I began going to private yoga classes with a teacher I knew. Again, these were covered, but what I'm telling you is, they weren't really free—as I was paying in other ways. Still, these sessions were the ultimate medicine—mentally, physically, spiritually. It was miraculous. I was able to actually do some version of this practice, which I had been quite immersed in previously. I had been getting somewhat close to what I considered an advanced point in this practice, and in fact, was seriously considering dedicating my life to it before my life changed. Now, going back to it in this more limited physical form initially caused me some regret, but when you really investigate the concepts of such practices, you discover the physical is the least of your goals. With most yoga, it does start there though—and I was in a condition to do be able to do so.

These sessions might have been once a week, but I would have gone every day if it had been feasible—such were the benefits and the ways in which the practice increased the faith and courage required to make it through. A further miracle of this voyage is that I have kept up this practice to the present day. I have gotten to a point where I can participate in regular classes and have been to many retreats. The true meaning of yoga is union or yoking your soul with God—let that be your practice.

You must live in the moment of difficulty in order to live in the moment forever.

What I mean by this is you must face tragedy as much as joy in order to live in the present. There is no night without day, and vice versa. If you don't put as much into solutions in all areas as you do into what you want, you will never reach true freedom. I can say such things now, even though I'm not certain I practise them. What this really means is to have no judgement—but back then, I definitely still did, and probably still do today. I would question what was happening instead of facing it head-first, I would try to be done with it as soon as possible in order to move onto something more useful. I stress this so you can try to find as much in the broccoli as the ice cream.

My mobility was far better at this point and I only used a cane. My need for accessibility was vastly reduced, so it was now possible for me to visit more places, which meant becoming more familiar with the Annex and surrounding neighbourhoods. This led to more reconnections with my tribe from before the accident. Though I still wasn't in the same reality, it was a great amount of progress and achievement to be able to move about more freely. My fear surrounding previously routine activities like walking was disappearing. Less fear always leads to more freedom, and I was becoming ever more certain I would one day return to the truth.

It was a time of gaining more independence in the areas of everyday necessity. This included things like cooking, shopping, laundry, housework, and general self-maintenance. These were all things I took for granted before, but nothing can be taken for granted with this level of injury—and I was indeed fortunate to be able to regain these skills, as many aren't. None of these things were easily regained, and they had to be done in a different way, which, at times, wasn't exactly pleasant. But it had to be, so it was.

The new treatments continued to show results, which was always encouraging, and I had to learn about taking small steps—both literally and figuratively. The yoga was the best of this, though I definitely wasn't certain about having the capacity to progress in it. As time went on, though, my flexibility improved and the impossible became possible. That is what yoga is inherently about—not just being able to stand on your head! In terms of my interactions with those appointed to be around me, I can't say they became smooth or easy, but they were definitely more tolerable. I suppose I came to realize they were just doing a job, and perhaps they realized that about me, too. Unfortunately, I wasn't completely convinced, so there was still tension with it on some level.

Perhaps they knew the situation wasn't entirely reasonable, and that was a factor in things improving. By this time, I was having deeper discussions with my lawyer regarding possible outcomes and the processes involved. I was getting a more detailed picture of what, exactly, I would potentially be compensated for, how the numbers broke down, and how they would arrive at those numbers. This was an education in itself—I was completely unfamiliar with this sort of thing, and, on occasion, I looked forward to these meetings, as they provided another viewpoint, and as far as I could tell, things seemed to be headed in the right direction. I wouldn't say these meetings were exactly pleasant, and I still didn't agree with the process, but they were useful and necessary.

At the time, they secured something for me called a non-earner's benefit, which was based on my previous income. This was definitely a good result. It gave me confidence there was an end in sight and provided incentive to carry on. I don't recall exactly how much this benefit was worth each month, but it was definitely useful, as I had new costs in this new life. For instance, a cane might break and there would have to be another immediately, shoes had to be of a certain quality in order to provide the support I needed, more space was generally required in places I chose to go, and my most regular mode of commute was now car. These were aspects of life I had completely taken for granted previously, as I was able to function reasonably well with the most basic of physical comforts. In fact, I can recall walking across downtown barefoot on several occasions! You really don't know what you have until it's gone.

I'm pointing out these details to show there were good things happening and that constant adjustments had to be made. Perhaps that's true for most, all the time, but I specifically remember it being a constant reality to navigate at that point. I have focused on my more challenging and unexpected twists of fate in order to hopefully educate you on what to avoid—mostly because that's where my learning came from and continues to come from for me. If I were to paint only a pretty picture, why would you believe any of my conclusions? Unfortunately, this isn't the made-for-TV version—I encourage you to give up on that. No, I'm giving it to you straight—or at least, to the best of my current knowledge. This perspective is the only thing that has kept me here up to this point and the only reason I have anything of any use at all to say in these pages.

I suppose it must have been at least six months or more I had been living there by then. Everyone I have mentioned had moved on. I had more reunions with old acquaintances, who were almost back to being a part of my regular life, though in a different capacity, and I also had increased communication with my family and meetings with them in the city. Throughout the good and bad, however, I had a growing sense of unease, a sort of dissatisfaction with the general direction of things. I suppose the correct term would be pressure—the type only the falsely accused would know. I was living with this and was uncertain of when it began to overtake all my other issues. My need to break free was becoming my priority. So, what do you do when you can't actually *leave* a situation? That was also one of the rules of the game—that I was supposedly not able to travel.

Well, all I can tell you is what I did.

CHAPTER 5

Avalanche

If you know, then you know.

Words will not be enough to accurately describe or capture the content of this chapter, but that's what's available. These words will be but a guide, a beginning—only a glimpse of the very tip of the iceberg of what really happened. Words can only create a shadow of an experience perhaps only a chosen few will pass through—and even fewer will be fortunate enough to tell the tale.

It started out innocently enough: a brief call to a long-lost compadre. *Can you get it?* and *Are you up for it?* were all that had to be said. It was on. My version of the games were about to begin. Let them have theirs—I would have mine. And I did. The problem was that someone had changed the rules without informing me. I used to see these brief departures from reality as useful, as a method to provide a glimpse of something more tolerable. Whatever it was, I used to be willing and able to return to the reality of Monday morning—whenever that turned out to be. That's not how this weekend went.

It was May of 2013, not long after the first very brief attempt at rehabilitation in Guelph when I was kicked out after calling the doctor a Nazi—this was in response to him saying to me, "Oh, you're from Jamaica... I know how you guys are". This time, I was necessarily escorted directly to my second attempt at rehabilitation, most likely still intoxicated from God knows what for God knows how long. As a matter of fact, only God knows exactly how I got there. This time was different, though—it *had* to be. There are many lines one crosses in the dance with the devil, the journey into the realm of ghosts and down the street of shadows—most of them imagined, but a few real. Most of them aren't even realized until the smoke drifts away—the haze of madness. However, on one of those rare and brief occasions, I did somehow wake up to the truth that something far greater than what could ever be documented or measured was now at stake: in a word, authenticity.

If my existence up until then had meant anything at all, it was as living evidence it was possible to show up in this world as yourself and remain so. There were rapidly becoming too many occasions where I had been close to sacrificing myself and the distance between *Not in this lifetime* and *I can't believe I just did that* was becoming perilously narrow.

I could tolerate the material destruction, any amount of loss of the respect of others, the several mortgages on any possibility of a future or any other versions of hitting rock bottom. You may have heard of hitting rock bottom, or watched it on the latest episode of *Intervention* or your favourite daytime talk show. All these things can be recovered, and I'm not certain how much they're really worth in the first place. If you go against what you know to be true, what gifts you were born with and have continued to be revealed over a lifetime, I don't know that there's any recovery from or appropriate rehabilitation for that other than death itself.

It was in one of these moments I realized, conclusively, that this ride was over. It was time to hit the very next exit—this was a dead-end road. Not because someone said so, damage to another, some legal mandate, or anything else I could blame in the future. No, the person I was on the verge of becoming was unacceptable. Even with lies, there was no justification. Nothing else I put in my body was enough to numb this revelation. That was the point of no return.

So, how exactly did we get here? Well, it definitely wasn't a straight road—it seldom is, and I'm definitely more one for the scenic route. Let me take you back, way back, before any injuries, lawyers, liars, dollar signs, or lives signed into and out of existence. Let me take you back to that time in my life when living was just living and tomorrow was yet to happen, and there was the idea of becoming something more.

There had to be more to life, all of it, than we had all been prescribed, and I was determined to find it. As I saw it, one of the most direct routes was what most call *drugs* but which I came to understand as *medicine*. Medicine for the sickness brought on by the fear fed through so many mass media tubes. Medicine to remove the blindness from illusion and consumption. A tonic to stand up straight in an upside-down world. The anti-venom to survive and thrive in a sick world. You see, I wasn't seeking escape but a way forward, into the new world. If the conscious mind could only acquire what it could grasp from daily reality, and that reality was false, it made perfect sense to attempt to gain access to other ones through various other states. To me, there was no sense of danger in any of this—at least not the form of danger one should run from. It seemed far more of a threat to remain sane in an insane place. This was choosing life, as I saw it—or at least a vital ingredient.

This particular journey began at some point after I had moved to Ottawa to go to school at Carleton University, back in the early nineties. I always knew this was part of my destiny—only, the correct environment was required for it to begin. I've heard that many have a great fear of venturing into these realms; for me the opposite was true. I always had a drive to seek the unknown, to move on from the conditioning, to break the bonds, to be reborn within this lifetime. There was never much around me, since my early days, that inspired belief, loyalty, or adherence to tradition. All the names, titles, labels, expectations, and obligations were illusions, figments of another's imagination or dream—certainly not for my benefit. They all had to be broken free from in order to find authentic life. Practices outside the norm were frowned upon—never discussed or even mentioned. The forbidden had to be explored.

It also happened that all the drugs I found some level of solace in, some notion of a path to follow, or which helped me feel I really knew or had mastered something, also contained components of "losing your mind" to varying degrees. This seemed to be a vital ingredient in every recipe for actualized living. Sounded good to me.

The voyages—or as most might call them, experiments—began innocently enough in the Ottawa days. In my eyes, a bit of the holy herb posed no risk at all. Being born in Jamaica, this particular substance was promoted as having a sacred quality, as a means of communication with the higher realms, a direct way to shatter the walls of Babylon. If you don't know what I mean, just go listen to some Bob Marley songs—and not just the ones on the radio or that your mom knows! This was my first step up the chemical ladder, as it were—the first journey to the other side of the tracks, the first trip to see if the grass really was greener. Being in university, of course, just about everyone I knew was accepting of this particular type of indulgence or any other form of escape, "partying," or "rite of passage."

I never saw my way of using it to be in any of these categories, but it was a shared ritual, and it perhaps played some role in the creation of a community which may not have otherwise existed—who can tell really. At the time, all of this was so accepted and routine, but it was still completely illegal. To me, that was part of the attraction—part of a new world being revealed. That was almost more intoxicating than the substance itself. The legal or "straight" world was all about safety and predictability—two things I had little use for. Always at the heart of it, though, was the idea of *going somewhere* rather than *escaping* somewhere else. I have found that if you are escaping, you run forever—but if you're progressing, you travel forever. So that was the idea: to travel, to find out what was really in the world of mind, not just what I was told about it.

At that point, I had yet to discover the magic of physical travel or come to know that one's mind eventually becomes the world. Being in a university environment was a trip unto itself. There was some amount of learning from pages and classes, but it was more about the totally new environment. I ultimately fell in with the guitar-playing crowd—as opposed to those who graduated on time with no debt, a degree in a major relevant to their career path, and a firm five-year plan. Somehow, this was never my concern. I don't know if I ever learned anything more practical than the minor pentatonic scale, and I definitely can't tell you anything from a textbook. There was a point at which I started to get serious about academics, but by then, the die had been cast, and to this day, I haven't completed that course of activities.

I did graduate with flying colours from becoming a stoner guitar player, though—after all, that is what I was actually studying. I was mostly a student of Herbs 101, but occasionally did venture farther afield into psychedelics—and more rarely into mild chemicals and, even more rarely, the devil's dust.

On one of these detours, back when what was known here in Canada as "raving" was still popular, we, the riders on the storm, partook of ecstasy for the first time. For me, it proceeded to be one of those moments in time where it seemed there truly was still hope for humanity and all dreams were possible. Some define these as one's "moment of arrival" in the scene, when you come to know why others get into and continue with this sort of lifestyle. Whatever it was, it worked, and yet another lane was added on what then still appeared to be the highway of discovery.

This is how it typically goes. When you're still at the stage when it seems like you're opening the doors, all you want to do is crack them open as wide as possible—at least I did. My ecstasy experiment continued after leaving Carleton to go back to Toronto. Friends of mine graduated, and I left for other reasons. Free of the burden of responsibility, with going to the clubs all weekend still being the thing to do, that was what we did—a lot. Perhaps I was the only one who never wanted Sunday to end. I still saw these times as a great communal experience—what everyone should be doing. It was what was missing from general existence.

Sometime around then, I received what most would consider a reasonable sum of money from a death in the family. I can't recall what it went toward other than this type of undertaking. That, perhaps, should have been an indication there were issues involved in my use of drugs, but it wasn't. It was still about the search for authentic living, to go past what I had been taught, to know something more than the North American capitalistic urban construct that led to complacency and regret as far as I knew.

This is what seemed to be happening, but then again, how would I know, since I was pretty much high all the time? I can say the MDMA (ecstasy) culture at least had the illusion of utopia, and it was as close as I could get to the hippie lifestyle of the sixties, which I always held in high regard and drew much inspiration from. In the dim light of Sunday morning (or sometimes afternoon or evening), when these excursions ended and the fuel ran out, the movement didn't really continue. Everyone would generally be on their way to whatever made the weekend possible again. There was no commune, farm or Volkswagen bus to go back to. There were always new and strange substances to try, though.

If memory serves, there were several forms of ecstasy around—of which I always partook—and there was always the herb to cool things down near the end, along with some concoction of sleeping pills. There was methamphetamine to keep things moving for some, but I was never into it—I probably only took it a few times. The Colombian marching dust was somewhat taboo, but available, and I can't say I was against it. That was a different realm altogether, though, that could lead into darkness and ego, which is what I looking to transcend. I may have taken ketamine a time or two, but again, that was an entirely different path. There typically was lighter fare, such as psilocybin, too, which I also mostly avoided due to its typical underworld itinerary. The fact is, at some point or another, I did take all of these—more than I realized, since no one really knows what goes into what you take. Alcohol and cigarettes, to me, were child's play—no danger or mystery involved, too easily available, just another tool of the masses to take you only far enough that you could still make it to the office by nine on Monday.

I can't really say how this routine ended, just as I can't say much about exactly why it started. It just sort of faded away—I suppose for many reasons. On some level, it was all about the drugs, and on another, not about them at all. What I can say is that most of those great connections that seemed to have formed don't exist today, and the visions have remained only visions. I personally have no regrets, however. I know the reasons I participated, and no great tragedies occurred.

During the haze of these years, I tripped into a whole other level of experience with the introduction to festivals—or more appropriately, gatherings. These were attended mostly by what I call blackbelt hippies: the ones who appear to have graduated from the weekend to actualizing Monday Morning someplace other than a downtown office.

It was a revelation the first time I arrived at one of these, about four hours north of Toronto, deep in the woods, away from civilization. Ozone summer in late June in the early 2000s. Where had these magical beings been hiding? I saw many scenes spread out across the fields I had always imagined but never knew actually existed. At least, not in this part of the world—and definitely not in this current time. I had only ever witnessed anything like it in Woodstock documentaries, and as far as I knew, it had been long gone as any type of living reality. Well, here it was, in front of my eyes. I had hoped to stumble onto such a treasure for a long time, but had no notion the event I had whimsically bought a ticket to because of the flyer art would be it.

This was part of the unconscious evolution of visions into reality. The most accurate description I can give is a Western tribal gathering combined with technology. We were all there. Yoga people, Rasta people, people people, pure hippies, techno hippies, ravers, what appeared to be North American Sadhus, those just there to "party," even authentic Hare Krishnas! There were about three to five thousand of us in total, all in a blissful departure from everyday attachments, possessions, and obligations.

Or perhaps this was their everyday! Was such a thing possible?

I took this all in when I arrived, wondering what was in store for the weekend—or the rest of my life. As far as I was concerned, there was no going back to normal after this. What did the medications have to do with any of this? Well, they played a significant role leading me to this destination. I was also to find out that unless one had a rigorous spiritual practice, some type of departure from the conscious mind is required to remove oneself from the consumer, fear-based, media-corporate construction fed to us daily and which most born in North America consider to be normal. This occasion was what I had in mind when speaking of progress rather than escape—this was not the all-weekend brain-frying that leads you to actually trap yourself further in what you were running away from, like the hamster on the wheel that can never get out of its own way. This represented hope, dreams, possibility, a taste of true freedom. There were many workshops and unofficial tutorials during moonlit banter about methods to liberate oneself—these ranged from tantra to yoga, traditional Native American practices and ceremonies, tribal drumming, and many other ancient and new-age practices. There were also the psychedelic schools: LSD, psylocibin, DMT, *Salvia divinorum.* All the modern versions of these were connected to raver culture, which owed a large debt to the hippie culture of the sixties. MDMA, though it didn't completely take you to the other side, was also a tool for many to seek the authenticity they found lacking elsewhere.

I can't specifically recall what I consumed or practised that weekend —probably as a direct result of what I did consume or practice—but that weekend directly led to a change in my lifestyle, relatively instantly. I ended up attending that particular gathering approximately ten years in a row, as it became a ritual. I went on to introduce it to many others who have said it opened their eyes to a whole other world.

Osho put it like this:

"Those who are courageous, go headlong. They search all opportunities of danger. Their life philosophy is not that of insurance companies. Their life philosophy is that of a moun-tain-climber, a glider, a surfer. And not only in the outside seas do they surf; they surf in their innermost seas. And not only on the outside they climb Alps and Himalayas; they seek inner peaks. But remember, one thing: never forget the art of risking—never, never. Always remain capable of risking. Whenever you find an opportunity to risk, never miss it, and you will never be a loser. Risk is the only guarantee for being truly alive."

Osho was a great teacher, who I've heard died addicted to nitrous oxide, and at one point, had a fleet of Rolls Royces somewhere in the region of two hundred. The point is that once one moves past fear, there are no limits—and the only way to do that is to become aware of your-self as an entity that does not contain it. That was my view on chemical enhancements at the time.

Immediately after the festival, I began to pursue the connections I had made there—those who had attended or, rather, participated for many years, or who had been pursuing lifestyles related to the general ethic that existed there. Essentially, there was a far larger group outside the event itself. It was far more than weekend hippie commune—it was a temporary nation.

This led me in many directions. One of the most notable and immediate was when I was at a local farmer's market one day soon after and came across an older gentleman who I had had a lengthy conversation with on the banks of the river there, while we had both most likely been in the throes of some altered state. He was dressed as—and seemed to be—a police officer at the time! This time, he wasn't—at least, he was not *dressed* as a cop. He was conducting his business selling wild, foraged produce at the market. Within about five minutes of meeting again, he offered me a job running his stall. Of course, I never mentioned anything about looking for employment, so how he knew I was available is another question. You see, these types don't really exist in the world of time and judgement—more on the plane of instinct. I was there doing some regular shopping, but I did have a lot of free time. I accepted in less than five minutes, which perhaps suggested I was as crazy as him, because I had no idea what was involved at all, beyond the obvious.

This seemingly random event led to an adventure in the Toronto health food industry for the better part of seven years! I continued on in various capacities during that time, with many employers and owners, most of whom I remain in contact with today and who I have come to know as mentors and friends. The point is, where else would this happen? Would this have ever been possible in the regular world of resumes, endless applications and interviews, countless volunteer hours with no result, and the like? This person knew virtually nothing of me, and my "resume" was whatever I said in that river talk and the five minute follow-up interview at the market. Yet he turned over his remarkably profitable enterprise to me for at least one day a week at the time. I could have taken off with the cash at any point—which, at times, was quite sizeable—and he would have had no recourse. I, too, knew nothing of him other than from those brief meetings. He could have turned out to be a maniac capable of God knows what. He did turn out to be a maniac, but he was not any typical manifestation of a "boss," either. I had been somewhat looking for typical employment for a while, then, with no result. But when you take fear out and put trust and faith in, these are the things that can happen.

I earned enough from doing that job—it really was much more than that—to travel to Thailand for three consecutive winters. I have since never gotten a job I've applied for—they have all manifested through some other channel. That is the case with this book, too. Your life is your resume. You don't have to earn a living—you're already alive—simply *live*. The miraculous is supposed to be routine—and it actually is, when you have the right eyes to see it. The ridiculous is meant to be normal and the everyday not to be so. But you can only see this from the other side. So, I would suggest a trip there by whatever means, if you haven't been. I'm currently looking to return myself.

Beyond that, my network in Toronto expanded to include many in the worlds of drum circles, the roots reggae community, the many other worlds of art and music, the discovery of the urban island oasis of Kensington Market, and many other fringe movements you might imagine. Basically, a whole new Toronto opened up. What can I say? You open your mind and the world seems to follow.

Things continued to expand in these arenas—most notably the farmer's market. I moved on to other posts around the city, and my job rapidly became a full-time position. This fell right in line with the evolved lifestyle I was seeking. Those established in this domain practised the philosophies I had been finding—most obviously in the intake of real life energy in the form of clean, living food. This was opposed to the intake of polluted energy in the form of profit-driven, processed food available for mass consumption. The former path could elevate you to higher levels of consciousness and real living, while the latter would only assist in bringing your energy down, keeping you stuck in the rut of everyday life (similar to being stuck in line at the grocery store, which was a place I rarely had to visit anymore). In this sense, you could say I was now hooked on organics! It wasn't completely about the changes in actual physical nutrition—but more about going further down this path that had opened up. This was simply the latest card on the chemistry table, yet another step on the ladder—chemical and otherwise. *Let thy food be thy medicine and thy medicine be thy food.*

After some amount of time, most of my days consisted of some type of work in the farmer's market circle, in which I had become somewhat well-known for being good at sales. I had the ability to move between many positions rapidly, and often accomplished what was asked of me. Evenings would generally consist of regathering with some of the same comrades from the day and progressing into some form of musical or artistic activity. I tended toward drumming and guitar-playing myself. There was a legendary weekly drum circle, which we all gathered at ritually and tribally to shake off the worldly shackles. This was yet another way to journey further upward and to discard the lower realms of the ego.

I find you really can reach elevated levels of trance when participating in drumming. With enough practice and repetition, and the right alchemy with other factors, I found it possible to get to a point where the mind was no longer present. You simply become the drum, the dance, the trees, the tribe, the sound itself. This is not a state one can predict—it simply comes about when the time is right, and when you get there, you're gone. There's no more time. I was discovering that this was the goal of it all—and to be able to get there without any additives was certainly better.

For me, the music became a substance unto itself—most directly, the drums. I had been previously unfamiliar with this instrument, but then began gaining experience with the Djembe. At that point, I was learning the discipline of keeping a rhythm in these large circles, as well as learning different rhythms. To tell you the truth, after a while, I didn't even know where I would pick things up. They would just enter the drum it seemed. I eventually became that guy going around town with a drum on his back. I never reached the master level of my comrades, but I could definitely keep a beat.

The other addition to the human laboratory was the guitar, which I had been familiar with for a long time. That's a bit of a different journey than the drum—a bit more of the world, I suppose. I was going around with one quite often, too. Basically, if I wasn't with one, I was with the other.

This may all sound like hippie talk—because that's exactly what it is. I had stumbled upon some new version of the movement. Headquarters:

Kensington Market, Toronto; time: some point in the early 2000s. These were heady times—daily living had become a peak experience in all the ways I've described. Basically, I was going on the wings of the wind from one revelation to next, with no goal or plan. This was where all the experiments had led... to the point of getting out of time, to being in permanent practice. To pass on the messages and shed the layers as you go. Medicines and various concoctions open this doorway of wisdom, then you have to walk through. It seemed as though I had stepped on through, indeed.

I cannot lie and say I had reached a point of purity—purity of heart and intention—but I would still partake of the elixirs. It was all a part of what was happening—not some sort of illicit, taboo pursuit. Everyone had their preferred flavours, and it was all in the spirit of communion and evolution. In the tribe I was part of, it was mostly the sacred herb in all its forms and strains, though every now and then, the psychedelics would reappear.

I can recall ketamine making its way into the rotation some point in the mid-2000s. I'm not quite sure how this came about—I believe it had to do with the popularity of the music associated with it back then. It was actually intended as a tranquilizer for cats, I believe, but it was associated with particular forms of electronic music. Now, I cannot reasonably come up with a way to put this one in the category of "medicine." Try as I might, it is a pure chemical, and doesn't really open any doors. In fact, it can close many quite rapidly. It simply showed up and was part of the scene, and didn't seem to cause much damage. Being a bit of a space cadet was part of my purpose at the time, and I saw it as useful and necessary to explore all avenues, as all of them were leading to the ultimate path. I wasn't under the illusion they *were* the path themselves.

I can also recall journeying with the cacao bean for a time. This is what chocolate is created from, and in its raw form, it is far more potent—and definitely is a medicine, far removed from what most have come to know as candy. This showed up in the process of working in the farmer's markets through an establishment called Chocosol, which got the beans from Mexico, I believe. In their raw state, these beans can bring on a high vibration. They contain theobroma, supposed to put one in an empathic state, and the beans also provide a lot of energy—far removed and much more balanced than that of typical stimulants, such as coffee and sugar. As far as I know, they were revered in ancient times for their ability to ward off hunger and to boost fuel for battle, similar to its coca relative. I can attest to most of this, after going through a few journeys and fasts with it. I definitely put it in the category of medicine, and still use some milder forms of it today.

There are many other superfoods I became familiar with during these years. They included blue-green algae, spirulina, wheatgrass, sprouts, goji berries, the durian fruit, and many others I can't recall. Essentially, I discovered when food is in its pure, natural state, it serves its true purpose as real nutrition, and provides life energy, as opposed to being some type of sedative—as can be the case with more typical, mass-produced food. It actually brought into question what food actually was. I discovered much of what is labelled as such is closer to the category of drugs, and much of what gets labelled as drugs are, in reality, food.

These are the days, those were the days, they will be the days, this is the day.

Up until this point, most of the experimentation had been just that. It was mostly a belief there was a whole other level not being revealed, something far beyond the physical, just beyond the veil. A strong faith, yes, though it was yet to become a knowing. Well... little did I know.

It was an exceptionally lazy post-festival day—and that's saying a lot for a bunch of burnt-out hippies hanging out in the middle of nowhere with no authorities around. I can say this because I was probably one of the most burnt ones as well as being among the laziest. All of a sudden, someone we all knew was casually offering around DMT. This was tantamount to perhaps finding a bag full of thousand-dollar bills , being offered a dream job by a stranger in the street, being struck by lightning and not dying, or some other twist of fate that only happens once in several lifetimes. Maybe like seeing a shooting star or snow in Texas. This bolt from the blue arrives, and one isn't quite certain which step to take next, because based on all appearances, things will never be the same, and you don't exactly know if that is positive or negative.

You see, DMT, in its authentic state—which we were assured this was—is no walk in the park. It is meant to be the deepest of dives into the very heart of creation. This is the one I had only heard about, alongside its cacti brother and ayahuasca relative. You couldn't buy a ticket for this—it could only appear like this, and it would be gone again, just like that. This was the top of the ladder, the king of the jungle, the top of the stalk, the hardest apple to get at the top of the tree that gets all the sunlight.

But would I actually partake? Or would fear take over? This was meant to remove all fear, of course. With that, I bought the ticket. Preparations were made. It was not an event to be taken lightly—there had to be white-glove service. A certain pipe, a specific method of intake, a hammock, a dose of trust, and a dropping of all expectation. That was the price of admission. This was a ceremony of the highest order, and we were in the Ontario "jungle."

So, we had lift off—the concord to the cosmos took flight. The proceeding fifteen to thirty seconds—or lightyears, depending how you saw it—confirmed all I had read about and had been preparing for. All of it was training for this. If you've seen an Alex Grey painting, this was inside one. I became the sun and the stars, the trees, the rivers, everything. The ultimate state of safety and protection. A world beyond the eyes, all in perfect kaleidoscopic symmetry—a symphony with no need for sound. It left absolutely no doubt all was well, always had been, and always would be. The worlds underneath and above this one were revealed in crystal clarity. This was like the very peak of the LSD experience, only far more tangible and detailed. This was not a drug—this was medicine, communion with all that ever was and could be.

Where do you go after that? Well, you just keep going forward—but with a new set of eyes. With less doubt and fear, a certainty there is something far greater at work, and a sense of purpose in passing on this information to all, and to play some role in getting this world on course to its highest potential.

To this day, I am astounded that, in real time, that voyage was no more than thirty seconds. There has yet to be anything to match how profound it was. Yet it is not something I crave. I can recall being in the clouds for months on end afterwards. I returned to my daily routines as they were, but with a firm commitment to stay the course wherever it led—because there really was no beginning or end. Now, if I see any type of art depicting anything remotely similar, I automatically know the inspiration for it and that someone else has glimpsed the beyond.

I made a commitment sometime around then to only participate and commune with substances in settings of a ceremonial nature. The days, months, and years carried on in much the same fashion, working with and spreading the word of the good food, becoming ever more engrossed in the music, going ever further down the festival path, building ever-stronger bonds with the Kensington tribe. Basically, spreading the vibes and following the sound. There weren't any more astral travels to speak of, but I did reach the mountain peaks of pranayama and glimpse the distant realms of yoga and meditation I had only heard of. What I found was that all the teachers I've mentioned have a different voice, but say the same thing... You're not what you think you are. It's gonna work out. It's gonna be cool.

I suppose you could say I reached my official blackbelt hippie status. There was no ceremony, though —and a good hippie doesn't really wear black anyway.

In June of 2010, I was considering moving to British Columbia to be closer to the essence I was seeking as opposed to constantly fighting the tide of urban "progress" in Toronto. Or maybe I would study jazz, or perhaps go to India and throw my passport in the Ganges.

"Life is what happens when you're busy making other plans."

This was when I woke up in the hospital. Lennon's lyric turned very real.

You've heard what took place then, but for the purposes of this chapter, what matters was me being put onto painkillers, steroids, and who-knows-what-else as treatment. Whether or not this was necessary (which it most likely was), it began my unconscious descent from the snow peaks of enlightened vision into the domain of ghosts and shadows. From there, proceeded a litany of prescription changes until I arrived at a combination that could take me through the return to independent living—and the ensuing dramas I have detailed here.

Then, there was that fateful phone call I made, precipitated by an endless frustration of dramas. It was my intention to only leave 'that' behind for a weekend, move into something more real to me and return to the routine afterward, as had been my practice before. My choice for this, if it actually was a choice, ended up being cocaine—I believe, unconsciously, I chose it because of its numbing properties, and perhaps the fact that it didn't take you too far out (at least not as far as I knew then).

I believe I had somehow become used to being in an altered, purely chemical state due to the medical procedures and medications. I hadn't done this dance too many times—I could probably count it on my hands. This time, I was aware of the origin of this substance from the coca plant—and that and its outlaw association had appeal for me. I don't recall anything remarkable about that fateful weekend other than when Monday came around, I wasn't done. This was sometime in early 2011, and I wouldn't be done until arriving at rehab that day in May of 2013.

So here was Monday. Whether it actually was Monday, I cannot say, but it was the day I had planned to return to my regular activity. But something said no. Carry on, it said. The hell with them, it said. OK, I said. "OK," said the voice on the other end of the phone—whoever it was this time that could make the arrangements. There were slight variations on this theme daily, for approximately two years. Eventually, I would conservatively estimate my habits reached the hundred-dollar-a-day level. I say "habits" because they ended up encompassing a whole range of abuses. What happened was, I morphed into an addict—and whatever was around ended up being consumed in that storm. It just so happened that some substances were far more dangerous than others.

The coca was always at the top of the food chain, and took priority above all else, hence the name "Cocoloco," which I bestowed upon myself. It started out being the first thing in my morning, and at some point, I couldn't sleep without it. Since cocaine is one of the strongest and most expensive stimulants on earth, that should give you an idea of how upside down things got. Imagine drinking about twenty espressos just before bed and you'll have an idea of how much my tolerance had built up. At times, ketamine was in the mix, alongside various prescription drugs, alcohol, marijuana (which I could no longer call the holy herb), MDMA, food, the Internet, pornography—whatever. There were also bouts of manic shopping for things I had no use for and (which are probably still in the box). There was a time when I bought heroin—but I somehow had enough sense left to know there was no coming back from that, and flushed it. The hard drugs are the most obvious and extreme, but it became more about the obsession and not being able to use a reasonable amount of any particular substance. Addiction is when you no longer have control, willpower, or judgement—something I could otherwise label as possession. Those who haven't had this problem will have no understanding. It would just be impossible to them.

I'm not proud of any of this—it's just to give you a real sense of what happened. I can recall waiting for endless hours outside a dealer's door with no response. This was the same house where I would repeatedly hide in the bushes in front of a church while waiting to be picked up to go back to Toronto in the middle of the night. I would spend days on end in that house, among people I didn't know, who had also been there for days. Meanwhile, the owner had probably been gone for days. All of this seemed completely reasonable at the time. The cocaine paranoia happened there routinely—many people looking behind the drawn curtains every five minutes, swearing that there were cops. There was the basement scene of wasted video game marathons among people who appeared from who-knows-where, remained for days, and left in a similar fashion.

These were the shadow people, who existed only in darkness, literally never surfacing from the basement. They always seemed slightly dangerous to me, but nothing ever happened. Their habit was video games, I suppose. There were the times in the bathroom when random women would come in and lock the door and describe what they would do for what I had left. How they came to this, I wouldn't know—or, for a matter of fact, how they knew I was in the bathroom. I guess everyone was in there the majority of the time, actually.

They seemed to believe they had some leverage in these negotiations, but I was only willing to consciously participate in *my own* destruction.

Despite—or maybe *because of*—all this, I would regularly start out there on a Friday and remain until the middle of the next week at least. Then, there would be the debate of how best to transport the load of whatever I was taking back downtown. The usual method would be spending a ridiculous amount to take a taxi all the way back downtown, which was about an hour. For the duration of these trips, I would remain hidden, head down in the backseat. This is the level one gets reduced to when in these circumstances, and it all becomes normal. I was like a dog chasing its own tail: what is inherently unfulfilling can never fulfill you.

There were more close calls than I care to remember during these escapades. I'm pretty sure the cab was speeding most of the time. At least twice, there were police roadblocks right outside the house. It would make sense the house was under surveillance, because the driveway was always full of cars and these types of scenes and activities were not occurring anywhere else in the neighbourhood, as this was suburban Toronto, where people went to escape the madness. To the trained eye, it would be obvious unusual activities were taking place there. The house was actually owned by the occupant's father, who I believe was told his son was in finance of some sort—at least, that's what his business card said. Judging by his son's ability to keep everyone coming and buying, despite his consistently inferior product and ridiculously high prices, he probably should have been. I suppose the crowds came for the atmosphere rather than the food.

I often wondered why I kept going. Misery loves company, I guess. It's also all about location, location, location—and convenience—when you're dealing with illegal goods. You also couldn't beat the perks: fellow crackheads, well-dressed, in order to maintain the illusion of sanity, an empty room to crash in as long as you continued to get high (which gave one the ability to overhear the events taking place with various women and the "owner" in the next room). And you would have the place all to yourself when he left for what was supposed to be thirty minutes—but could be eight hours—plenty of time to wonder who was coming to kill you!

The most noticeable turn of events when I was living in my apartment on Bloor St. was an incident involving a noise complaint and police. By this point, I had my fingers in many fires, going in many directions at once. The days were the nights and the nights were the days and it was all a daze. I was more or less a pharmacy unto myself—and the evidence was there for anyone to see.

At some unreasonable hour, came a loud knock on my door—the type of knock that tells you there's a problem. Then the words, "This is the Toronto Police, open up." Already intoxicated, I figured this was the end, and pretty much started having a panic attack. "Just a couple minutes!" I said. As I was frantically (and I hoped silently), systematically hiding the evidence, which was scattered everywhere, I figured it must have been obvious to them what was going on. I will never know why they didn't insist on me opening the door faster or enter themselves. After far more than a couple minutes, I went to the door to accept my fate.

"We've been getting noise complaints," they said.

"Oh, my apologies," I said, "I guess I didn't realize the time." In fact, I didn't. "It won't happen again."

With that, they were off, without even coming inside. Unbelievable. I can't recall exactly what I did next, but I know I didn't stop the lifestyle I was living—though perhaps I became a bit more careful. I didn't know it then, but all these escapes were the hands of angels upon me. Back then, I might have just called it luck. But think about it: my building was notorious for criminal activity, and the one time the cops came, it was only for a noise complaint. On the lighter side were the shenanigans of leaving paraphernalia in the bar where my yoga teacher worked, literally running around getting high all over town, frequenting local strip clubs at first call, and finding creative ways to finance my habits including becoming familiar with pawn shops and cheque-cashing places in order to use funds intended for other things. It goes down and down, this slippery slope.

"Guide and protect I 'n I, O, Jah Jah, through
all these stages." – Bob Marley

"If Jah didn't love I, if I didn't love I, would I be around
today? Would I be around to say?" – Bob Marley

"Listen to Coltrane, derail your own train... well,
who hasn't been there before?" – Sheryl Crow

The snowy slope is slippery, indeed, and you don't know you're sliding away until it happens. You have to learn how to stop.

There was endless sneaking around, constantly looking for a bathroom—as a matter of fact, I wouldn't go places unless I knew their facilities were properly situated and laid out in such a way to facilitate my practices. This is one's priority when under the influence. I've often wondered since how to harness this power in a direction with some actual possibility in it. If humanity could figure that out, we could all walk on water. Such is the power of that demon. People will literally do anything to get what they want and believe they need—myself included. I was in no financial position to carry on like this, yet I did, through some mysterious force of desperation.

There were times all my connections would run dry or disappear, and somehow, I would find another—literally within a day. And these people don't advertise. It was quite incredible, actually, in a ridiculous and unfortunate way. Somehow, I could sense it in the air. I wasn't the worst, by far. I hadn't yet descended to the pipe or needle—but I certainly was on the way. I imagine that, for those who get there, these scenarios are multiplied tenfold. By this time, there was no more glamour, no more living the "high life." It was now work, simple and plain: how to get what I now *needed* to get on with the day.

At some point, these chemicals do become a requirement for the body to function. Opiates are more noted in this regard, and I don't have that experience, but a similar phenomenon does exist with coca after prolonged abuse—and I can tell you the mental withdrawal is no joke. I experienced this on the few occasions when both cash and contacts ran out. Climbing the walls for three days straight without leaving an infested bachelor apartment is no joyride.

I was definitely at the point of realizing that this was a losing battle, and completely unsustainable in any way. It's set up for you to lose—you can't beat the house. It's all organized by billionaires out there profiting off your demise.

All of that was well and good, but once you're in it, you're in it, and the point comes where you can't live with *or* without it. Until an answer comes, all you can practise is harm reduction. In the horns of that dilemma is where I stood. In the meantime, I did much more harm to myself.

From a practical standpoint, the most obvious risk of my destructive behaviour was the jeopardy I was putting my legal case into. Each and every substance that I took would make the process of reaching sobriety longer and less likely. At some point, I would be made to state my case in relation to the accident, and if there were any trace of intoxication in me at all at that time, the opposing side would take that and run with it as far as they could. They would argue that I had been a user at the time of the incident, and therefore was at fault, making no settlement necessary.

None of that would have been true, of course, but they don't deal in truths. And the truth was that they *would* have an argument if things didn't change. I can remember detoxing myself before one of the pre-liminary medical interviews—or, more appropriately, interrogations. This involved somewhere around a week of switching to caffeine as a substitute, climbing the walls again, not sleeping for days—basically, attempting to function as a sober maniac. After a while, the insanity of sobriety can outweigh that of addiction. Nevertheless, I made it through the insurance-appointed neuro-specialist's questioning, and as far as I know, there was no report of drug abuse or "questionable" behaviour. I'm quite certain I went on a run after that, but the job was done. I suppose at the time, I wasn't far gone enough to completely disregard or forget the reason I was going through all this destruction.

Other low points included the times I waited at a south downtown location to score repeatedly, with a sense of real trepidation, but also combined with anticipation of a positive outcome, and hoping not to have to do so again—at least for however long the budget would allow. There were many other close calls with police—that lifestyle is a constant cat-and-mouse game with the law, and there is always the sense it's almost over (which, in turn, creates the desire to use even more). So goes the hamster on the wheel.

By far the worst result of my transgressions during these times was the loss of most of the great friends and real community I mentioned earlier. Irreparable damage had taken place. I've made amends with all those I can but there doesn't seem to be any going back. So it is.

Through the years, I've found out life can't be bought—but it can be lost and those losses are irreplaceable. One time, right after cashing one of those cheques meant for something else, I went to use the funds and it was no longer in my pocket. It was at least two thousand dollars, as I recall. Karma's a bitch, I suppose—or maybe it wasn't such a good idea to be walking around with cash in a notoriously bad neighbourhood, or maybe it wasn't such a good idea to be cashing cheques in the first place, to "need" such amounts of cash in the second, or to be using hard drugs in the third. Once you've crossed the line, there aren't any good ideas, because your mind isn't your own. Ultimately, this period of my life cost an amount in excess of a hundred thousand dollars.

There were times I would get prescriptions for the sole purpose of trading them for my medicine or finding a way to get invited to houses where I knew there were medications I could either use or trade. I would think more than twice about these undertakings, and I believe I only stole someone's medication once, but that is where things were—and they weren't headed anywhere better, because this sickness is progressive. There were times I was intoxicated in places I swore I never would be, among people I also never believed I would be. There's the untold damage I know I did to my digestive system, and most likely my brain— and who knows what else.

All of this and far more are in the job description of a full-time addict—and that's what it becomes: a job, with no perks or benefits or future. How many senior drug addicts or dealers (after a while, they're two sides of the same coin) have an ounce of pride about it? If they do, it's only because they've learned to lie so well they don't actually know they are anymore. I know that's where I was—and I am still coming out of it, on many levels.

The fact is that the entire lifestyle is a lie—including the notion you have to go outside yourself to find whatever it is you imagine you require (which, in truth, is nothing at all). Ask a baby about it. In fact, outside of yourself, the only people you should ever seek answers from are those speaking nothing more than unintelligible gibberish, because that will prove far more valuable than the words of so-called teachers. The truth will not be in words, as they are only a guide, much like a map. I believe it is said that if you find someone professing to be the Buddha, you're supposed to kill them. I also heard it said that "the road of destruction leads to the palace of wisdom," or something similar. I don't if I've arrived at any palace, but I do know I was on the highway of destruction.

If you're going to sell out, at least get good value. There's no return on investing in narcotics. Just listen to more Coltrane and Miles Davis.

I won't lie and say it was all bad, because nothing is, and if it was, no one would do it. And it did give me a story to tell. There was the honeymoon period, when it seemed like I was winning, getting away with murder. I was literally in the clouds for a month or two, and if it had been possible to stay there, I still would be. There isn't enough money in the world to keep you there, and if there were, you would die first. In the beginning, your tolerance is high, the consequences are low. If the lights stayed on, no one would ever stop. Why would they?

The thrill of the lifestyle is actually more intoxicating than the chemicals themselves: living as an outlaw and getting away with it. There was also the newness of it, associating with a different crowd, running around all over town. All the things you'd heard about and imagined to be worth it. And we had our moments, but that's all they were—nothing permanent, of real value. To get that requires something more than a dollar. And you tend to get what you pay for. One thing I can say now is that I know the reality from the fantasy.

I'm still here to tell the tale. Many aren't.

Somewhere in the midst of all this, I went into rehab the first time at a place called Homewood in Guelph, Ontario. This must have been sometime in mid-late 2012. I can't really say. Somehow, the insurance and my doctors worked it out, apparently, since I wasn't on earth at the time and had little capacity to do much.

I was in the throes of destruction then—firmly in the eye of the storm, unable to live with or without it. By that time, I had confessed everything to most parties—especially to those that could do something about it, because I certainly couldn't. I was in the fortunate position to have funds available for rehabilitation due to insurance being involved in the legal case.

I'm quite certain that on the ride there, I made about ten bathroom stops—and it's only an hour drive. I probably don't have to explain why. Upon arrival, I threw what I had left into the bushes in front of the building. I might have had some deluded plan to carry on using while I was there. This is the brilliance of addict logic. I genuinely had the best of intentions upon being admitted—but I've heard that makes good pavement for the road to Hell.

Things were going along reasonably well until I was being interviewed by the head doctor, who asked me where I was from. When I said Jamaica, he literally responded, "Oh, I know what you guys are like."

I don't know if you're aware of the stereotype of Jamaicans in Toronto, but it isn't good. And I imagine it would be worse for someone in rehab—for cocaine. I believe the words "you Nazi fucker!" are what immediately passed my lips. So, this is what I was getting into? As far as I can recall, some debate was had about my admittance at that point, but things proceeded. There was some sorting-out of roommate issues—my injuries made it impossible for me to have one—and this chapter began.

My only experience of rehabilitation had been the show *Intervention*. This place seemed to be as advertised. There was some minor conflict in the first few days regarding the schedule and the fact I considered a bathrobe appropriate attire for breakfast. Apart from that, I felt good connections being made between myself and the fellow clients, and I saw potential in the process.

They didn't, apparently. After what appeared to be a positive first weekend, I was informed first thing Monday morning that my time there was done. *WTF?* I was certain some evil villain was behind this, intent on fulfilling his stereotypical belief. Such is the world—which is why I have no use for it. I let the whole place know this, in no uncertain terms, and I'm sure they haven't forgotten—but it made no difference. There was no explanation, and that was it. He and they are the ones who have to live with it—

It isn't hard to guess what happened next.

I started making calls to my connections before even leaving the facility—most likely, I made arrangements for that very night or soon thereafter. I sincerely hadn't planned it like this. I had hoped to come out of there a changed person, on a path with some potential other than premature death or prison. In these sorts of unfortunate scenarios, a common lament is, "If you don't stop you're going to die," or something close to it. To me, this misses the mark. Dying is the inescapable reality for everyone—so how can that be a reasonable argument for anything, really? It makes sense to whoever says it because they most likely aren't the ones hurtling toward it at lightspeed.

A stronger argument would be that the person is no longer living as their authentic self, and that the path they're on will only lead to worse pain and suffering (most notably for them, the one consuming poison on a regular basis). As far as I'm concerned, the greatest struggles arise when one can no longer see a path to authenticity—not what happens when it's all said and done. We all have that to face. I certainly had reached that point and was now far past it.

There isn't always a way out. I had now made an attempt to change but met with the powers that be. I've been offered the theory I wasn't actually done—that I hadn't hit the mythical rock bottom everyone has heard of. Perhaps not, but as far as I knew, I was finished with this death-style—it certainly could no longer be called a lifestyle.

When you're a full-blown narcotic addict, the chances of stopping on your own are low—otherwise, everyone would do it. And if people were really self-reliant, they wouldn't be drawn to drug use in the first place. So, that was the state of things: no way in or out. I suppose you do what you know until you know something else. With that, the search was on for another place to seek rehabilitation.

CHAPTER 6

Bottom of the Ninth

"When you got nothing, you got nothing to lose." - Bob Dylan

Strike one was Homewood, strike two was the realization the insurance wouldn't last forever. I would have another hearing at some point, and at the rate I was burning through money—and myself—all would truly be lost. This had to work. Even though I was now blind, I could still see that.

I have learned through this that when an entity gets to the point of morphing into its opposite, it has run its course and no longer serves its intended purpose. Coca showed me this when it became a sleeping pill and started to cause the same problems I initially believed it solved. When your favourite food makes you sick, when the Rolls is stuck in traffic for an hour or the Ferrari crashes and someone dies, the doctor tells you that you have to quit sugar and your wife gets pregnant again and is consumed with even more fear, or you're smoking ganja for breakfast... such is the futility of the senses and the yin/yang of all things. If you're going to participate in the merry-go-round, beware what's really going on—and that you're gonna fall off, too. The higher you fly, the harder the crash. If you're gonna do it, *really* do it—eyes wide open, headfirst. But realize that none of it is the thing—*you're* the thing. Stay the course.

One more thing... if you're going to sell out, don't be cheap. Don't go for the bargain basement price of obligation, expectation, attachment, tradition, fear, or other false advertisements and marketing ploys—because that's all they are. A low price has a high cost. Most will go for the nine-ninety-nine special—but don't. It's an illusion. Go ahead, find that extra penny and get the real thing. You'll have to replace the budget version repeatedly, as it continues to fall apart in front of your eyes. Yet somehow, you go for it, again and again. Pay the price for the full value of spirit and truth. It's guaranteed for life, and there's a strict no-return policy. If you're going to join the world and its soap opera, only go for the highest standards. Drugs aren't one. *You* are the drug, and every need's got an ego to feed.

On May 13, 2013, I arrived at Bellwood Health Services. I was picked up by one of their staff—which should give you an idea of the type of isolation that had occurred. I'm certain the drive there was quite surreal on both sides, but I can't recall precisely. Immediately upon admittance, I had interviews with staff and doctors about how, exactly, I had gotten to this point and what, exactly, this point *was*—in terms of what I was coming off, how long I had managed to stay clean, how long the whole thing had gone on.

This was familiar territory to me after having been through St. Mike's and Lyndhurst. Institutions were fine with me. My problem—or at least more of them, were caused by the outside world. My only issue was having my own room, which I knew was a requirement for me based on my previous experience. As far as I knew, insurance had figured that out, but I believe they said they would try it for a night or two the other way. It probably had something to do with the concept of humility—but that didn't work, as I had predicted.

I wasn't certain what exactly I was in for, but how bad could it really be? Just a bunch of out-of-control maniacs living in a hotel together without escape, right? It wasn't the stereotypical, idyllic rehab centre you've seen in the middle of nowhere, with rivers, streams, and horses. I requested those, but apparently my case didn't have that value, so insurance didn't go for it or doctors wouldn't sign off on them. I suppose you have to be hooked on way more for a lot longer to get coverage for those. This was in the suburbs of Toronto. At least I was headed somewhere, even if I didn't know exactly where. The other way was definitely heading nowhere fast.

I don't know what happened those first few days other than figuring out the room situation. I do know that I had an intense drive to leave during the first week—and technically, the doors weren't locked. But what was there to go back to, really? Apparently, not much, since I didn't do it. I was told it was withdrawal causing this—which would make sense, because previous to this, I would stop only if I literally *had* to (meaning, no money or connections). More than that, this was an entire shift in lifestyle—because even before I went off the rails, I was a dabbler for a much longer time. So, this was some sort of chemical homesickness.

After that passed, I had to get accustomed to actually having a schedule—which had definitely become a foreign concept. In the world of addiction, your drug of choice makes the schedule. As my memory serves (which has also most likely undergone untold damage from my uses and abuses of substances), the day would generally begin at some hour that, to me, seemed obscene, with a staff-appointed volunteer duty—typically involving making breakfast or organizing of one of the various meeting rooms for an hour or so.

Eventually, everyone there would do all these duties. My choice would most typically be the interior design as opposed to going to battle with the coffeemaker at an even *more* ridiculous hour. Part of the effort there, though, was to change one's attitude from that of complete indulgence to one that served the collective—so at times, I would deal with the coffee. After all, addicts are addicts, and nothing would take without that caffeine!

It was always quite strange to me that clients were allowed to continue smoking and drinking coffee there, which are also hard drugs, but just happen to be legal. In my estimation, most wouldn't go if these were banned, too—but probably, the combined effects of withdrawal from both of these *and* the narcotics would cause mass death and rioting. I guess people have to be allowed *something* for their money (which was no small amount, though I only cared to investigate it far later).

Following this would be a communal breakfast, at approximately 8 a.m., which I have to say was quite good. These daily culinary events were probably the highlight for most, though they came with the possibility of introducing yet another addiction. Following this, on weekdays, was group therapy, which, apart from sobriety itself, was the highlight of the entire program for me. A small group of clients would share their various accounts of the dramas and destructions caused by their habits—including but not limited to cocaine, heroin, methamphetamine, alcohol, marijuana, sex (though these clients tended to be isolated into their own program), gambling, shopping, people (otherwise known as codependence), food, video games, the Internet, innumerable prescription painkillers, ketamine, countless opiates, and uppers and downers of all sorts. If it existed, it was apparently possible to become addicted to it—to the point of having to go to an institution to be instructed how to deal with it.

There were also the stories of the matching dramas and destructions that had *caused* these habits in the first place. It was hard to say which was more colourful or more accurate. It was definitely a privilege to be part of this group on a daily basis. The topics of conversation were light-years removed from the forced, obligatory banter of daily existence. It is rare to get to these levels with anyone—much less within the days it took place in that group. That was one of the advantages of residing in what was rapidly becoming known as the Bellwood Bubble.

Some were hesitant to get to the real dirt, but I had already been doing that, as I didn't hide most of my habits from many, as long as there was no legal consequence. I saw no shame in being a drug addict. I didn't see it as being any worse, for example, than being a banker, lawyer, polytricktian, or fake estate agent. I saw no shame in my lifestyle and had no issues until it became a death style. My issue with narcotics is not moral—it's simply that it's misguided and strictly a no-win situation on all sides. The house is completely stacked against you, you will never reach your imagined destination, and the risks are nowhere close to equaling the potential benefit. More simply, this juice was definitely not worth the squeeze. The best way to stop: don't start. If I could still partake and not have to consume everything in sight, proceeding to lose everything of real value, I probably still would from time to time.

It is necessary to remind yourself of the beauty and mystery within and without, lest you become attached only to the gross material and the daily grind, as it has come to be known. But there must be a reason for it all—otherwise, our petty life takes over and pretends to be the reason itself. We are capable of far more than this. You demean yourself by staying only in that mode. Get in to get out. There are far more reasonable methods to access the other side. Begin that journey. Have no shame in yourself. You are simply you. Shame and guilt are worldly productions. We do not arrive here with them. And it probably isn't the best idea to take them to go, either.

We would discuss when and how our habits started, different situations that led to or exacerbated them. Various consequences over the course of our using careers would also be debated, along with our unsuccessful attempts to stop before arriving there. There were many routes that led to the final destination of surrender, but the common crossroads was a state of being totally out of control, unable to proceed in any direction. I found out there were many methods through which people arrived at Bellwoods. Some were sent by their employer as an ultimatum, by the judge as an alternative to prison, by their wife or family as a plea or last resort, and more than a few by the military, because of the PTSD that led to even worse destruction. I took it as a badge of honour that I was there of my own volition and hadn't been forced by anyone, offered any sort of deal, or had to be intervened upon. Yet the choice was clear. My advantage was having insurance to cover the costs—which many, unfortunately, don't. And there was of course the settlement deal that was in jeopardy, and the deal I'd made with myself that I was going to see this through until the bitter—or, hopefully, *bittersweet* end—which was also now in doubt.

Consider everything it took for *you* to get here... to be reading this, right now.

> "And if you buy the bullshit, then don't lose
> your receipt" - Damien Marley

The therapy group continued to evolve and grow as time went on, and the sharing got deeper and more revealing. The use of substances seemed to have begun for everyone with a genuine search for something more but ended up in a place of far *less*. And now, we were stuck in neutral or firmly in reverse—me included. It became more remarkable as time went on, and my illusions concerning the nature of addiction were shattered as a new education began.

Immediately after the group were the doctor's lectures, which lasted about an hour. These covered a wide range of topics, from a clinical perspective on the roots of addiction to the various effects of different substances and behaviours, to how to navigate life after achieving sobriety. All the doctors specialized in the treatment of addiction. Most of them had also published books on the topic—so you can see how this was like going back to school, the major difference being that the only examination was on youself.

These talks were another highlight of the program. I discovered the scientific side of the disease of addiction—which is what I found out it actually was, contrary to popular opinion. Some get it and some don't, and it's not a matter of choice at first. It becomes a choice once a solution is available, but prior to that, a true addict doesn't possess that luxury. I had always seen it as a matter of willpower, and thus had passed judgement on others until I arrived there myself. They explained there was a point at which the body came to *require* the chemicals—much like it needs food—so by then, some literally cannot stop by themselves, even if they want to. The effects of untreated withdrawal could be severe or even fatal. There is also a section of the brain that becomes so captivated by the particular substance or behaviour that it can be equally problematic to control. All this was news to me.

My main habit had gone on for approximately two years, and I considered that to be quite a while. But it now became clear why others struggled far longer—especially if they didn't have the means to pay for appropriate rehabilitation.

Things are seldom what they appear. Remove the mask.

At the root of all the lectures was the insight that most if not all habits begin as an apparent solution but eventually become a problem in themselves, while the original issue still hasn't been dealt with—in all likelihood, it has gotten far worse, due to neglect. So, the real solution was to clear the deck and find out what the issue was in the first place, the theory being that a person at ease would not have a desire to escape themselves. More often than not, this road led back to some sort of drastic, untreated trauma an individual simply could not overcome. This made perfect sense, even though it wasn't my story. My factors were a bit more complex than the typical client there. It wasn't a straightforward scenario, as my route had been from casual user to full-blown addict mostly due to the effects of major injuries.

As it was explained to us, most are never able to consume any amount of their drug of choice that relieved what it was they were suffering from. It was a revelation to discover it had nothing to do with ethics, discipline, or willpower of an individual—but rather the damage done by a particular event. The doctors also went into graphic detail when discussing the long-term effects of the most commonly abused substances, of which cocaine was always near the top of the list—typically up there with opiates, most notably heroin. Their descriptions of these were truly horrifying. Most revelatory here was that the substances that are legal and thus considered less risky and more acceptable actually could cause equal or *far worse* damage. I will not easily forget the images of lungs blackened by cigarettes and what I personally witnessed of a peer experiencing alcohol withdrawal.

Following these sessions would most usually be lunch. This was one of the required three to four meals a day—which was apparently how the majority of normal, functioning humans operated. This was quite a shift from ingesting cocaine as a "breakfast of champions all-day buffet", then consuming only what actual food was necessary to keep one alive until they had more. It's known among veteran users that the effects of drugs are much greater on an empty stomach—and who had time or resources for something as trivial as nutrition anyway? The cocaine diet wouldn't appeal to many, but the illusions took over and it began to appear as food.

The culinary experiences were the only tangible possibility for one to really indulge themselves during the program in a way that would be deemed acceptable. But acceptable to who, exactly? Was an ice cream overdose any less of an offence than a narcotic relapse? Under no conditions I have come across can one create a reasonable argument that cocaine is a necessity to sustain life, while it doesn't take much of an effort to create such a defense for food. Nevertheless, both can be abused and cause severe damage to an individual. The very first second you intake even one grain of cocaine, it is excessive and abusive, while with food there are endless shades of grey surrounding the question of sustenance versus indulgence. I imagine the answers to these ponderings lie within each person—these questions most indulged in continuously, as I certainly did. Put a bunch of addicts without drugs around uncontrolled food (or anything else with the remotest sense of satisfaction), and it will certainly morph into a drug of (lack of) choice in short order.

A prime example was when there was a cocaine or financial shortage, I would substitute with espresso and coffee. If there had been a way to create a rehabilitation program that included constant fasting, I'm certain that would have been done—but we would've found a way to get uncontrollably hooked on that, too! What I'm getting at is that any activity can be used for an inappropriate purpose. Food is meant to be nutrition to provide energy in order for one to live, but in most of the modern world—or perhaps more accurately, the North American world—we have gone far past that. It is then easy to see how a powerful attachment can develop, though I once scoffed at the apparently ludicrous notion of a food "addict" or an actual condition called an eating disorder. When I was living on welfare in downtown Toronto sometime in the early 2000s, this notion would have been *truly* laughable. I was hustling around to whichever church was open for a free breakfast! Yet here I was, sitting literally beside a table of a group of peers in the eating disorder group. Interestingly, this group was isolated, along with those with an apparent uncontrollable sexual dysfunction, as they had to be separate from the rest of us, the "normal" drug addicts. To tell you the truth, I'm still not completely sold on the notion of sex addiction, either. If virtually every human act can be labelled an addiction, are the only options for everyone to be constantly in and out of some form of rehab, or else to seek monastic life? These are the questions one ponders while in such an environment, because the whole concept of addiction and its only logical progressions of early death or sobriety lead directly into the philosophical arena in terms of one's purpose to begin with.

At this point, I was approaching a month there—which meant a month of total sobriety from all non-prescribed drugs and alcohol.

According to Wikipedia, "Sobriety is ... considered to be the natural state of a human being at birth. A person in a state of sobriety is considered to be sober... In some cases, sobriety implies the achievement of 'life balance.'"

This was the first time since my very early days at Carleton, most likely, that I had been free of all substances for such an extended length of time. It was definitely a rebirth of sorts. A death of the lifestyle that had me heading to an early grave and the birth of one that had perhaps never existed—one free of attachment to the past, that might actually have the possibility of a future. Contrary to popular belief, getting sober does not automatically eradicate all damage of the past and magically place you on a magic carpet ride through the rest of life. It simply makes the rest of that life actually *possible*, allowing a chance to repair the destruction done during the illusory years and to create a second act.

I've heard it put forth that once you get clean, that's it: chocolate falls from the heavens, trees bear dollar bills, and rose petals cover the floor perpetually. This has not been my experience, nor would that be of much benefit to a true addict—which one remains, by the way. What does magically happen, though, is the disappearance of your desire or imagined need to escape yourself in favour of acceptance of your true self—the one that has been covered by the dust of the world, of so-called teachers, of the well-intentioned but ill-equipped parents and all the rest.

It appears to be only we humans who go on the run from ourelves, yet end up going in circles, searching for a treasure that is already there, but too close for us to see with open eyes. The birds, the trees, and the flowers know it—so follow only them. Eventually—or perhaps immediately—you will see everything was always there, but no one ever gave you the keys or an accurate map.

The baby knows this before it is covered by the names, expectations, obligations, plans, hopes, and dramas of one who calls themselves a parent but is so in name only. A real parent knows they do not possess anything—much less a child—that the child is here for them just as much as they are for it, and that maybe *they* have found *their* teacher. They also know not to put any limit upon their baby, so as not to create more limits. They would also know they alone are not responsible for this creation—that it just happened to come through them, and that they are just simply there to allow their baby to fulfill their own destiny, not to be a vehicle for their own dreams (which they may not have been allowed to manifest due to similar disturbances). You will only see this—and many other things—by giving up the chase.

"Don't ask 'why addiction?', ask 'why the pain?'... In other words, addiction is a normal response to trauma." - Gabor Mate

I was now fully immersed in the program at Bellwoods. It was my new normal. Plans had to start being made about what to do after, even though the exact date had yet to be determined. As with my previous institutional visits, at this point, I would have had no problem becoming a permanent resident. Totally isolated from everyday life, philosophical teachings and debates of all variety, a unified purpose, no housework other than the morning duties, acupuncture, anger management, guaranteed socialization with other maniacs from distant lands—what more could one ask for? One problem: it was in the region of five thousand dollars a week (as I now understand). It wasn't coming out of my own pocket, though, so it didn't seem like an issue. I suppose the goal was to eradicate the problem so as not to lose it all in the end—so, in that sense, it could be seen as an investment.

Following that logic, it made sense not to return to the same environment once it was completed. One of the mantras in the recovery world is that "If nothing changes, nothing changes" and "The only thing that needs to change is everything." Simple enough. I suppose it also went against the philosophy of treatment to let someone stay for an indeterminate amount of time, lest the whole thing turn into another escape, or it be rumoured they were more interested in profit than helping addicts. At the end of the day, it was a medical facility and not a hotel (even though the building had, at one time, been exactly that!). A tropical vacation would have cost me far less—but I probably would have taken even more drugs and never made it back! So with that, the search was on for some sort of situation to go to that wasn't my apartment on Bloor Street, where all the temptations would still exist. I left that search up to those who knew how to do such things—and in fact, were getting paid quite well by me to do so, though I might not have been completely cognizant of it the time.

Some words about the concept of "recovery". One has to be careful when labelling or giving titles, lest the word serve a false purpose, leading you on a wild goose chase. To me, the word "recovery" has a negative connotation, implying going backwards, to recapture, while the entire premise of getting sober is to move forward. I have absolutely no interest in recovering any part of my life as a drug addict or what led to it. It's commonly understood that for an addict to use again is to die. So, my word is *progress*. While many may have conquered the worst and most fatal of their habits, they still succumb to milder forms of destruction and slow suicide, such as cigarettes, caffeine, sugar, and—probably most dangerous of all—requiring the approval and respect of the outside world. Some of this is in jest, but be careful what you label yourself, because it will become another identity you become. Be attached to nothing and available for everything. Remember what true sobriety is. So, *progress*—progress in all directions—is my word. Or, in the words of the original Rastafari brethren, "Forward evah and backwards nevah."

The most realistic possibility for housing post-Bellwoods was an establishment in Etobicoke, in the northwestern limits of the city, called NRIO, the Neurological Rehabilitation Institute of Ontario. It dealt with spinal cord injury (SCI) and Acquired Brain Injury(ABI) cases, and had sobriety as a requirement and charged an even more obscene amount I was also not aware of at the time. In addition to the general philosophical and spiritual concepts presented, I was introduced to the twelve-step model of sober living. I was vaguely familiar with the idea, and had attempted to go to at least one AA meeting during the fog of Bloor Street but it lasted only five minutes before I went on a rant attempting to justify the use of cocaine.

The version I had heard about was the traditional Alcoholics Anonymous one, which I can't say was too appealing. But here, I found there were all sorts of modern, updated versions, such as Narcotics Anonymous, Marijuana Anonymous, Sexual Anonymous, Codependents

Anonymous, Food Anonymous. Cocaine Anonymous, obviously, was the one I was directed to.

My previous, limited understanding of this particular brand of self-knowledge was erroneous—and had been based only on what was popularly recognized. I had a bias against it for apparently being traditional, rooted in traditional Christianity, which went against all my previous practices. I had no personal associations then. But then, I had never been a crackhead or run over by a car, left for dead, and lived to tell the story. I was very resistant initially, but I had to understand this as my new reality. In that vein, and with much heated debate about the concept of God, in combination with the reality that meetings were a requirement of the program and that I had come way too far to turn back now, I began to attend.

I don't know how much I was actively participating in the beginning, but I was there. I believe the requirement was somewhere in the region of ten meetings a week while in treatment, and ninety meetings within ninety days of initial sobriety, or "ninety in ninety," the notion being that it's one thing to stay clean in a bubble like Bellwoods and quite another to do so once you have your own keys.

Bellwoods was the beginning of journey into another new world—this time, of Cocaine Anonymous, the twelve steps I have continued to this day, and the results have been nothing but positive. So far, I have almost eight and a half years of continuous sobriety from all non-prescription mind-altering drugs or chemicals to show for it.

The cast of characters I came across there was an education in itself. There were the garden-variety powder cocaine addicts such as me, who had lost most if not all of their dignity, pride, and self-respect but managed to maintain other things, such as cars, jobs, homes, and in some rare cases, even a few relationships (other than those with drug dealers and Western Union). Then there were the veterans, who had been on this merry-go-round for far longer and were now possibly addicted to rehab, considering they came and went so many times. Then there were those with the needle—this is a separate road altogether, typically borne of years of struggle and ultimately far more immediately dangerous than where I was coming from, based on the stories I heard. You've probably never and will never hear someone casually say, "Hey, wanna shoot up?" This is a dark path I am thankful never to have stumbled upon. Then there were the opiate users who had more extreme stories than I did, because the nature of that particular substance seems much more seductive and thus harder to break from.

My main question with that was and still is, *why do people start?* Then again, why did I? I never had much common ground with the alcoholics, because that, to me, was almost like cheating. Where was the risk, danger, and mystery? It was far too tame an undertaking to ever attract me. Sure, after decades, you could lose your liver and acquire something called "wet brain," but what was that compared to riding the wild horse daily? There were also the more exotic habits such as ketamine, amphetamines, and fentanyl—which was just beginning at the time—and all the more modern "raver" drugs, which I wasn't familiar with.

By far the most confusing affliction to me was that of gambling, a sector from which a member of the therapy group belonged. All the features are the same as with the rest of the addictions, with the key difference that there was little to no payoff. I've even heard stories of people who have never actually won anything. At least with narcotics, you do stay high for a short period—there is some positive result from each use, no matter how minuscule. With gambling, it seems it's all about the *possibility* of victory, which the user becomes convinced is getting ever closer with each roll of the dice. The tragedy of this is that even if they do "win," it only increases their delusion and obsession—as with all habits when you "score." With hard drugs, it generally is a gamble every time you partake, and the entire lifestyle is rife with danger and could be over at any moment—which is part of the attraction. Actual gambling however, seems to be a whole other realm, not as fully understood by those looking to treat it. So, I certainly wish all the best to those who have that malady.

There were also the behavioural addictions, to things such as spending, shopping, gaming, Internet use... I believe I heard of one case of "love" addiction, which has to do with a need for people or relationships, as I understand it. I certainly had phases with most or all of these versions of "acting out," as it was sometimes described there, but I could not say I became full-blown addicted.

I did manage to make connections with most of the others who were admitted while I was there. Our common ground was that we all had some habit that got out of control, became unmanageable, and greatly disrupted our lives, putting the most valuable parts of those lives in jeopardy. For me, this temporary community solved, if only also temporarily, the issue of isolation, not necessarily caused by, but definitely exacerbated by, my lifestyle. Most addicts who have spent any consistent or repeated time using will tell you the party ended and it was them in an empty room doing what they did—and I was no different. It really was like revisiting my Carleton days—learning new things and becoming new in many ways.

This time around, though, it was addition by subtraction. There were no grades, and the only requirement was showing up repeatedly. And the diploma at the end of it was having a life once again. While there, I got along well with everyone, for the most part, other than a few early anger management issues (something I am still dealing with). I formed some new bonds, but as time has moved on, so have they and I. In some sense, I probably should have invested more in that bonding attempt but perhaps there were too many other issues on the table at the time. We weren't there just to socialize, and "real" life does return.

The most curious incident at Bellwoods was discovering one of my fellow clients was a police officer. This caused a variety of reactions when it I learned of this. All police were my sworn enemy at that point. It had always perplexed me how any sane human could willingly choose to become one. The very concept of dictating someone else's freedom or defending a broken system has never crossed my mind as a possibility for one second. How could anyone be convinced that there was any purpose at all in that vocation? It had always been painfully obvious to me that the presence of police does little or nothing to reduce crime, and they are no more than tools of the state.

Of course, fate would have it that I came across one in a place where I and everyone else were on a quest for self-improvement and wisdom. When I discovered this, I felt a sense of vindication or even retribution, since all my interactions with law enforcement had been negative up to that point. I believe I told this person exactly what my experiences had been with law enforcement when I saw them in the housing section of the facility. I realize now this was unreasonable, but back then, I was still in the throes of judging others and absolutely hating law and order. This fellow addict was not spared my wrath, whether or not they knew it. I have since found out the malady of addiction is one of the great equalizers. It knows no colour, race, or class. It will bring anyone down, from the highest peak to nothing but ashes.

The most typical solution—a dedicated spiritual practice of some form—is the *real* great equalizer, in my experience, in that it provides benefits to any and all, often leading to what is known as the "grateful addict" in twelve-step circles. This describes someone who has been so rewarded by sobriety and practice of the program that they no longer regret their time in Death Valley. I don't know I'm all the way there, but I do know that back in that environment, the police officer and I were equals. It was probably bad enough just being there for a police officer without facing critique by those supposedly in the same boat. Who's to say what type of officer he was or what his story was.

I've since learned through much error that it isn't my place to judge but to carry out my own destiny to the fullest, not interfering with that of another unless they ask me to. Though it is also part of my destiny to expose the illusions of this world, it seems to bear more fruit and to not get me arrested to do it this way. A key feature of the typical addict is a chronic inability to see beyond themselves, and I was definitely guilty of that back then. I am still not cured—it is an affliction that requires daily attention. I probably also had and still have residual resentment from the injuries. I have been in therapy of various forms for years, and most likely will continue for the rest of my life.

What else can I say about my eighty days at Bellwoods? Well, I definitely went in there one person and came out another. I must stress, again, that nothing about this was easy. But it did become far simpler once I accepted my circumstances and after the struggle of early withdrawal. It no longer seemed like such hard work—more like something necessary, worth taking full advantage of. I had definitely been uncertain it would be successful in the beginning, but as time went on, there was no doubt, and upon completion, much like with Lyndhurst and St. Mike's before it, I had the strong sense that any mountain could be climbed. The road ahead was wide open.

Before my accident, when I was a hippie. Around 2005.

This was when my name was Clarkie Roots. I had hair
back then. This was what I did all the time.

June 10, 2010 The Scene of the Accident.
(photo courtesy of the Toronto Metropolitan Police)

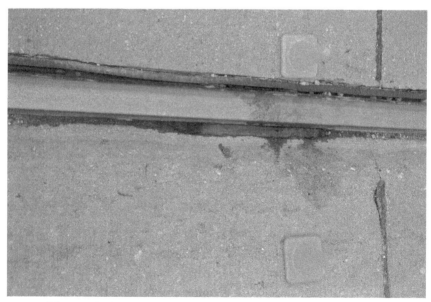

If this was the blood left on the road, imagine what happened to my head.
(photo courtesy of the Toronto Metropolitan Police)

I guess my head was pretty hard! You can see the flesh that got left behind in the driver's windshield. (photo courtesy of the Toronto Metropolitan Police)

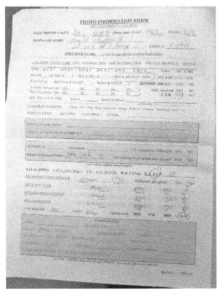

Police report: Interesting to note it was marked as "fatal accident from sudden death" at that point in time.

Leftovers. I still miss this hat... my life as it was before the accident.
(photo courtesy of the Toronto Metropolitan Police)

Hibernation. Winter, 2014.

It can be done! 2019

Rewards on the other side.

On BC Ferries between Vancouver and Victoria during the
pandemic lockdown while I was writing this book.

At home. 2021

Later can be greater. Enjoying a good time with Conrad
Novak, a friend from high school. 2022.

It's worth the wait. 2023

CHAPTER 7

NRIO or WTF?

"If there is no struggle, there is no progress."
– Frederick Douglass

Well, here we were, on the road again, this time from Bellwoods to the Neurological Rehabilitation Institute of Ontario (NRIO) — or more accurately, a lot further down the rabbit hole, perhaps even to the other side, maybe to the end of the rainbow.

I had been admitted to Bellwoods on May 13. I had spent eighty days there, so the day I left would have had to have been sometime in early August. On that day, as I was being picked up by a rather curious blonde lady, who I eventually found out was one of the higher-ups within the establishment, I remember wondering, *I got out of drugs, but what other insanity am I getting into now?* Was I to move on from the problems of the powder to just more human problems? Or would my stay here turn out to be a great success, as Bellwoods had been—further help in paving a way to the future that beckoned me.

Once again, this was still all an unfolding mystery to me, so my only choice was to go in headfirst, as I had with all the previous stops on the road. I had the very basic understanding that this place was for the treatment of individuals with brain injuries—or what are more commonly known as Acquired Brain Injuries ABIs—with the supposed specific intention of equipping them with "life skills" in order to function in the outside world once they and the other "supports," as they were known, were no longer available.

I was unaware I wasn't in possession of these necessary skills. As far as I knew, the main skill required for life was to live it, and as far as I could see, I still had that. I suppose the issue was that when you progress from a catastrophic incident to being an out-of-control, powder-snorting maniac, most may feel you have some issues with the typical tasks of everyday living. That argument might have been reasonable, but another large part of the reason I went there was that it would be another sober bubble. While pondering all this, I driven up to the driveway of what appeared to be some sort of mansion or hotel rather than a medical institution.

NRIO was another hub of sorts, in that most activities were centralized in one location, though the clients' movements weren't limited as strictly as they had been at Bellwoods. The focus there was improving the long-term possibilities for those who had somewhat recently suffered a brain injury. That meant the daily schedule revolved around what were called "life skills"—a questionable notion in and of itself. Their interpretation meant cooking, budgeting, various forms of education—related to brain injury and otherwise—and how to manage changed circumstances and find options in "regular" society. This was once again felt by the powers that be to be clients' ultimate goal—still a concept I had issues with. For the most part, things seemed to function based off the stated intention—as least as far as I could tell, anyway.

The other clients at the time appeared to be in a greater state of difficulty than me, with more severe and noticeable injuries, but I ended up getting along with them in a similar fashion as I had with the others at Bellwoods—perhaps for similar reasons, the most obvious of which was the disrupted futures we shared. Once again, it was an enforced commune—we were not all there by choice, but rather it seemed to be the best or most reasonable option at the time. I can't speak for anyone else, but I certainly didn't have another institution in the plans. I had gotten used to not looking too far down the road. I can recall many evenings spent debating how, exactly, we had arrived at this point—in addition to what we would do next—and complaining about the services and treatment we were receiving, even if it was five-star as far as rehab is concerned. I never did find out the actual incidents that had led to the others coming there, nor the specifics of their injuries. I suppose such things are better left unsaid. What was clear—and, far more telling—was that they had all been thrown drastically off course, and were looking for a new direction. There, we were dealing with a condition which had no cure, though—and yet affected every aspect of our existence.

At Lyndhurst, some had healed more than others, but there was typically a clear way forward, though it might be difficult and somewhat unpleasant. Meanwhile, Bellwoods equipped clients with a completely viable and immediate option once the program was completed. It was then solely up to those who had graduated to move ahead with the knowledge they had gained, charting a new course. With damage to the supercomputer, however, it is not such a black-and-white situation. There was no going back—and how do you go forward when you are quite literally not the same? Well, not to be a broken record, but it came down to taking the next step, giving my all where I was at the moment and letting the fates take it from there. In this case, that meant signing up for programs I knew I didn't technically *need*. The reality was, I still wasn't a free person in regards to my legal situation. I had to keep the bigger picture in mind while being educated on how to do the dishes and make coffee, among other domestic tasks related to dwelling amongst the living (which, as far as I knew, I already was, though the paperwork told another story). In such a quandary, all one can really do is maximize the opportunities available.

With that, I got into a rigorous physical regimen again, as I had at Lyndhurst, though not quite as intense due to the progress I'd made and my new environment. Along with that was a regular aftercare program back at Bellwoods, which I participated in fully as often as possible. I also signed up for guitar classes with a previous compadre of mine, which I somehow persuaded the higher-ups was necessary for any sustainable future for me, in addition to yoga and twelve-step groups. This was all successfully topped off with me eventually being crowned the in-house ping-pong champion!

The first order of business was finding the local Cocaine Anonymous meetings and implementing them into my schedule regularly. As memory serves, there were two in the Etobicoke area, and I believe I began immediately attending four times a week. With true sobriety, however, mere attendance is not satisfactory. Rather, active participation in the program is mandated. You must *inhale*—a concept all of us were far too familiar with. In essence, you had to go as far and hard forward as you had in reverse. With that intention, I set forth on the "real" twelve-step vertical journey outside the protective womb of Bellwoods.

However, I was still under the supposed protection and definite monitoring of NRIO, so I wasn't completely free. I had to be accompanied to these meetings initially—for what reason, I'm still not actually certain.

"Can't keep my eyes from the from the circling skies, tongue-tied and twisted just an earthbound misfit, I.

...

A soul in tension that's learning to fly, condition grounded but determined to try." – Pink Floyd

In essence, the twelve-step venture was a welcome departure from the enforced continued surreality of my current residence. In spite of the reality I was practicing, a concept known as harm reduction was promoted in those circles. That interpretation of "recovery"—what I label as *progress*—employs techniques to make continued usage as "safe" as possible. In my case, completely disposing of all the baggage wasn't an option—so, though I was definitely on the path of sobriety, I wasn't yet able to emancipate myself completely. So, though I didn't take any more drugs, I couldn't yet live my life fully. So, though I didn't want to be there, I had to be. Harm reduction it was.

On a fateful day early in my participation at meetings, I heard someone telling their story of recovery—progress—and it made radical sense to me. That man became my sponsor that evening, and continues to be today. He has become something far more than a mere friend. If not for that serendipitous period of exile at NRIO, and meeting that man, I would not be here today—because later on, he would make certain I passed through the crossroads.

The road is made by walking (Antonio Machado). Trust yourself—you made it this far.

I pressed on through the obstacle course. I created an additional hurdle by deciding to do away with caffeine—more specifically, its most notable and abused representative, coffee. I, like everyone else on planet Earth, was most likely a coffee addict at that point (though not of the variety that lines up at Tim Horton's ten times a day). This particular affliction began, as I might have mentioned, as a replacement when dealers, money, or both had disappeared—but it stuck around for the cleanup. Caffeine, as you may or may not know, is quite a potent stimulant that just happens to be legal. My theory on this is that it allows people to do whatever they do and still get to work on time. That and its similar chemistry to my drug of choice all played a part in my ultimate rejection of it. Little did I know, this was not to be without issues.

As you know by now, the addict world is upside down—day is night, night is day, and the sky is whatever particular colour it seems to be that day. It should come as no surprise to you—though it did to me—that the first effect of caffeine withdrawal is not being able to sleep, which I experienced continuously at one point for at least a week. For me, that was cause for great concern—but it held no great significance to the staff there. That should give you a reasonable picture of my environment at the time. There were possible other factors involved in my sleeping issues—with the most likely suspect being medication. But going even a bit more insane from the lack of rest was not without benefit—like delirium, hallucinations, had the added benefit of greater community acceptance! One would imagine coming off a stimulant would lead to further sedation, but I suppose I'd built up such a tolerance that it came out the other way. Next came headaches—which I never get. Mercifully, those didn't last too long. And there were other complications, like no longer being part of the daily Timmy's ritual.

This was another endgame scenario. I wasn't going back to it, end of story. And if something that is acceptable, legal, and literally abused daily by the masses can have such effects when it's no longer available on a relatively mild user like myself, what does that tell you about our supposed leaders? And if it can cause such trouble, what destruction does the coca god wreak? Again, this is what one has the privilege to ponder when not stuck under the thumb of their vices. The more freedom I gained, the more questions arose. You thus have what's in front of your eyes now.

Ultimately, the caffeine removed itself from my being without much more disturbance, and the eventual results were worth the struggle. As far as the other struggles, they continued. By far the worst and most unnecessary of these was the constant monitoring, chauffeuring, and chaperoning everywhere I went. A particularly striking example of this came at one of the Cocaine Anonymous meetings, which I remember being on a Thursday evening, hosted by my sponsor. I had to be accompanied to this meeting by one of the staff and, for their own reasons—which I will not reveal here—they took an interest in the topics being discussed that evening and proceeded to tell some of their own story during the sharing segment. Now, in and of itself, there is nothing wrong with this—but when you take into account the reason they were there, it definitely is an issue. She was not there as part of her own program—she was on the job, not seeking a solution to an issue with dire consequences. My issue with the whole thing was that I didn't actually require this "support" on any level other than paper, and that this particular individual had a front-row seat to what wasn't a spectator event. I wasn't showing up in their living room to discuss the more significant issues of life, like seeking a sustainable method to maintain one. The leader of the meeting eventually also took issue with the turn of events. I don't recall what the exact solution was, but it involved her dirty laundry no longer being aired unless she actually became a member of the group and admitted to having a substance abuse problem of some sort. This type of scenario, though not necessarily as dramatic as that, repeated itself on an almost daily basis.

It is necessary to understand I was and am a fiercely independent individual still invested in self-reliance—most importantly on the level of consciousness. That being what it was, I was forced to participate in elevator level small talk an endless number of times a day on drives to various appointments, at the gym and pool, and just about anywhere else you can imagine. On one of these all-too-long outings to the local grocery store, I remember purposefully hiding from staff for an extended period, probably claiming I had gotten lost. Perhaps this sort of thing was unreasonable, but the whole arrangement was literally becoming a bit too close for comfort. This routine was enough to exacerbate any condition I already had, and if I didn't have a brain injury already, it was more than enough to create one.

I am illustrating this not only to give you a picture of what was happening but to expand slightly on the topic of independence. Independence, in my current opinion, has far more to do with whether you can reasonably exist in your own skin than the conventional physical/social definitions. A common example would be "I pay my own rent" as a statement of autonomy. Paradoxically, I've found if your level of self-reliance is not in harmony with your material progress, it turns in on itself out of a need for companionship, support, agreement, lust, or any other manifestation of a lack of true self-confidence.

In the end, even though I was living in what some might call the luxurious NRIO, the systematic destruction and rapid regression in my ability to take care of myself perhaps played the most significant role in my admittance to a psychiatric ward on the exact day their program was due to end. I had develped a condition one of my doctor's described as "learned helplessness," and I would have to agree. Logically, the outcome should have been the exact opposite, wouldn't you say? Well, be careful what you assume and what you do with logic. Only request what you actually need and cannot provide for yourself, and then you will move out of the victim role and really become something of value in this world. To borrow another phrase from Osho, "The more you free yourself from yourself the more you become free for everything else." Well, that's not exactly Osho—there's a bit of me mixed up in there, but he wouldn't give a damn. To borrow from another master, Dr. Wayne Dyer, "You can't give away what you don't have." Conversely, no one can take away what you don't require. If I'm ok in myself, then I don't need anything, so you can't really steal from me. Ponder this for a moment. I will too.

Meanwhile, back at the ranch, things were more or less the same. Of note was that I had lost quite a remarkable amount of weight, which may have bee a result of the delirium from my lack of sleep in combination with my consistent exercise routine, which was the only method available to counter the twilight zone of my current non-fiction movie. Or perhaps I was hallucinating, and my body appeared different!

There was also the incident that left me questioning whether it was the staff or the clients who had the brain damage requiring immediate treatment and banishment from society. It probably had something to do with the schedule or the continued monitoring, and possibly some perceived act of incompetence of theirs in my view, since I had probably developed an ego issue from the amount I was spending and the number of people who were at my beck and call. Whatever the trigger was, whatever I was trying to do, or being told to do that I did not want to do, I transferred my message of frustration loudly throughout the entire house, which was no small feat, considering its size—it required several screams. The episode ended with me seeking relief from it all on the grass in the backyard, which everyone found quite amusing—especially my fellow clients, who recalled it regularly during the rest of our time. I'm certain anyone who witnessed this still wonders what possessed me that day. At that point, I was roughly three months through my stay. From the outset, they had made it clear it wouldn't be a long-term stay—which, in their estimation, was a maximum of six months. I considered this completely unreasonable, especially considering I was quite certain it would be a rapid descent the minute I left. It certainly was an extension of the twilight zone to be in a situation once again in which I was supposed to participate fully and engage with everyone as part of my general rehabilitation, but at the same time, be aware that once those six months were over, everyone would go their separate ways and, in all likelihood, never hear from each other again. The result—I was in a constant state of limbo. As friendly and apparently genuine as everyone (staff) was, they were all on the job, and the minute that was over, they would be, too. They all begged to differ, as those in such a situation are wont to, but time has proven otherwise. On this rollercoaster, I have observed that most will say and do absolutely anything to maintain their position or status. I happen to be one of those few that will absolutely *not* do that—which might have something to do with the fact that I've never gotten a job I've applied for. I believe this practice is commonly known as "saving face." I'm here to let you know no one can take your original face, and that there is absolutely nothing common about you. So, when you find those uncommon souls—or your uncommon soul—head that way. Take it from me: the finer things aren't things.

Generally speaking, NRIO didn't specifically do anything terrible, but I can't say anything particularly remarkable happened, either. In terms of bottom-line value, I would say it was definitely questionable at best. They did fulfill their end of the deal by ensuring I maintained sobriety, but at what cost? I don't live in the past these days, and dwelling on the negative only creates more of the same. However, this is a work on non-fiction, and I'm telling it as it was. The most concrete example of the unbalanced nature of my program was when I was, for all intents and purposes, forced to miss a great compadre's funeral due to the restrictions I was under. I don't want to place inappropriate blame here—over seven years have passed, and I'm doing all of this from memory.

To the best of my recollection, I did my absolute best to convince them and made all possible arrangements to attend the funeral, but at the end of the day, they saw going to Ottawa unsupervised with such short notice as too much of a "risk" and a deviation from routine for an exemption. Most likely, it had something to do with liabilities on their part, though I'm certain they would use some more creative language in their defence of the decision. But the fact is, I'm the one that has had to live with it, even though their mantra has something in it about the wellness of the client. But such is the life of an insurance plan. In other words, if you buy the bullshit, you better get a receipt.

In my opinion, the greatest risk anyone can ever take is not living while you're alive. This particular fallen brother and I certainly did a lot of living while he was here, and missing the occasion marking his untimely passing is something I can never get back. This is what I mean by real value. If I could go back, I would have said they could do what they wanted, but I was going. Once again, in the words of the natural mystic, Bob Marley, "You can't buy life"—or, in this case, the opportunity to honour one gone too soon in ceremony for the last time (in this realm, anyway). That twisted scenario is an accurate microcosm of the environment I was in. I'm not one to mourn, because what's gone is gone and what's to come is to come, and who is to say that the next realm is worse? Regardless, some moments are worth the price of admission. So, show up... Just show up, every time.

Walk a mile in my shoes and you might know about my blues. Since it would take me about an entire day to walk that distance currently, you might want to ponder that.

Despite my dissatisfaction with the restrictions I was under, there were also a few adventures on the positive side of the ledger. I had continued progress on a physical level—which is vital to any general progress forever, as there are no cures for spinal or brain injuries. I probably got to one of the highest levels of physical capability since the accident. I do thank NRIO for making that possible, but in my opinion, the physical only accounts for approximately one third of a human being. From what I've gathered, there is the physical and the psychological or we might say the noise in your head. But then there's also always that hidden third dimension that brings it all together, catalyzing the others. It's what essentially brings colour to this world. Call it spiritual if you like, but it's the part that is unchanging; it precedes everything. If I could venture a guess, it's what comes after and what you see when you can't. I've come to see that when you give equal attention to all three dimensions, the rewards are greater than the sum of their parts. It's when so-called miracles take place—and I can verify that they do, constantly. The evidence is in front of your eyes. But are they really miracles, or just a matter of appropriate effort in the right direction?

My time at NRIO also allowed me to continue in two programs at Bellwoods called "Aftercare" and "Relapse Prevention." I valued both of these programs greatly and don't believe I missed a single session during those six months. Both groups consisted of weekly check-ins in a supervised setting with clients who had graduated at a similar time but found it necessary to continue with some form of program.

The aftercare group consisted of each person describing their week in relation to "recovery." I found this type of setting endlessly rewarding and had absolutely no problem sharing. In fact, it would have been very simple to take up the entire session with only my stories. I've often been amazed to witness those who are unwilling or unable to do this. I have an issue with pointless, obligatory small talk about the weather, politics, relationship gossip, hockey, Britney Spears, or any other pointless dribble most regurgitate without even realizing it. How many actually mean what they say? Or don't realize it's actually dark outside when they say good morning? If you actually mean it go ahead with the good-mornings, go ahead—but if it's night, it might be good to say goodnight or even nothing at all—which doesn't seem to be much of an option these days. Small things become big things, and then you have the global drama that we all wonder about and question how it originated. In that group, however, every word was of great significance and most likely consciously produced, since there was feedback from the rest of the group if they disagreed or believed you were lying for whatever reason. This was known as crosstalk, which wasn't allowed in the twelve-step format. This led to some fiery debates, and I fully supported that. If you have nothing to hide, you have nothing to hide.

The other group, Relapse Prevention, was similar, with the exception that it focused on specific methods to avoid using again rather than a general recap of each participant's week. I found it to be just as useful as the other, and at times, even more so, due to the relatively early stage of my sobriety. All of this truth-sharing was a welcome respite from the non-reality of my daily existence.

But the reality was that it was all coming to an end.

Around the four-month mark, there began to be some mention of a discharge plan. I already knew this was coming, so it was no surprise. Their plan was that I would move to what they called a "more independent living" situation—which was another residence that belonged to them, not too far away, that was virtually unsupported (even though I recall it being called something that indicated the opposite). And it was akin to going from the Ritz to the Motel 6. I protested vehemently, but they insisted all would be fine, that it was the standard course of action for most people who passed through their doors, and that there hadn't been any issues in the past. I had my by-now typical routine of requesting extensions, with some modicum of success, but the die was cast once again. I probably got an extra month out of them at the most. After having been through this song and dance a time or two, by the time the day actually arrived, I was relatively certain this next excursion would not be one to write home about.

CHAPTER 8

Further Down the Rabbit Hole

There won't be too much to say about this fork in the road, because the sad but all-too-predictable truth is that it led to a dead end. The location after the main location of NRIO was called something like "SLA." It was a massive shift in lifestyle from virtual round-the-clock supervision by a complete staff to one person coming by for a few hours a day to make sure I was basically functioning—or, as I saw it, to make sure I didn't become a massive liability to their bottom line. That may be a bit harsh, and with hindsight, I can now clearly see it was all meant to be, but I didn't have those eyes then. I still had reliance on human aid in most matters—which is fickle at best. As a result, I was still subject to their frailties and whims.

These days, I put the onus on myself—and the force that created that self—when concerning the most significant of these matters. If you're going to put your faith in a person, why not put that same trust in your-self? They are no different from you. No better, no worse. I encourage you to do this all the time, though it is no small feat. If you haven't gotten to the end of the road and lost all hope, then gotten to the other side, it will be harder than pulling teeth to divest from the belief someone will be there for you or that you're not alone, when the stark fact is that *they might not be* and *we all are*. And there is absolutely nothing wrong with that. The quicker you get to that point, the quicker you will become your own master, and no longer be a victim of this world and its dance. Learn to dance with yourself, and then you can dance with anyone. Take it from me.

The rest of the details of this phase are superfluous, and I've grown tired of expounding on the negative. Let's just say it was a rapid descent into the heart of darkness, with me quite seriously threatening that lone staff member that I was going to jump into Lake Ontario in the dead of winter, along with my refusal to sign a bizarre medication contract (which I will never know who stood to benefit from—it definitely wasn't me). The train wreck reached a full stop at the Mt. Sinai psychiatric ward sometime in the winter—either late 2014 or early 2015.

Here we go again.

CHAPTER 9

Holding Zone

"To be on your own, with no direction home." - Bob Dylan

Well, what can be said about ending up in a psychiatric ward immediately after leaving a facility for neurological rehabilitation? Well, not much, really—other than what happened. What happened definitely wasn't in the plans—but neither was getting run over and left for dead, so there we go. I guess I'll just go from the start.

There comes a point where words have served their purpose and any more will only lead you in circles. I am almost at that point. If you have never been admitted to a psychiatric facility, it is quite problematic for me to give an accurate description of what it is like on the inside. Words are certainly just the beginning.

So back to what happened after I threatened to jump in the lake. I had a regular psychiatric appointment, during which my doctor interrupted proceedings to inform me I needed to be admitted to the ward on the same floor. Things definitely weren't the best, but I didn't see this coming. But when you threaten to jump in the lake, it would make sense something is wrong. I have no clue how such conditions are identified, but I guess that's why I was on the other side of the desk. So it was. Now, you might imagine such a decision would indicate a crisis was at hand that required rapid admission. Well, once again, you and I would both be wrong. "Admittance" apparently doesn't mean actual admittance, but being put on a list for a bed, *then* being admitted—a curious concept in itself, because not much sleep actually happens in such environments. Be that as it may, I was now waiting around in a second NRIO location for exactly that.

So, I was in another limbo session, which by now was old hat, but was nonetheless beyond tedious, because my time there was definitely over. And even though I was, in a way, looking forward to this next chapter, it is always better to dive in and get on with it. If I had had such a progressive perspective at the time, I probably wouldn't have been where I was.

I believe it took about a week to ten days for the space to become available. It could quite possibly have been a longer wait than that, but I don't exactly know at this point. When the fateful day finally arrived, it was beyond bittersweet. On the one hand, a tragic turn of events was over, but what was on the horizon wasn't necessarily a welcome shore from the tidal wave NRIO had turned out to be. Maybe the best way to put it is: imagine you're constipated and have to take so many laxatives it leads to diarrhea. Sure, one episode is past, but the next isn't what you might call pleasant. At the end of the day, the only saving grace was that perhaps this new route could actually lead back to a path of progress and sustainability.

And that day did literally take until the end of the day. The call came sometime in the morning, but all these permutations and possibilities led to hesitation on my part—mostly because even if you go into one of these places not knowing your own name and come out as Superman, it's not going to be a joyride. I was in a conscious enough state to realize what was taking place. Essentially, if you get run over and left for dead, and follow most of the rules afterwards, you're not supposed to end up in a place that seems further back than when the whole thing happened. But so it was.

Once I eventually got out the door, which was as difficult as it sounds, it was more or less a typical hospital admission. But I cannot express how different it was from checking into Bellwoods—that time hope reigned supreme. This time around, it was more like, well, what the fuck else am I going to do? I don't know that I ever found out the official reason I was sent there, but I would guess it was something to with my threat of suicide—I only made it once, but perhaps that was enough. In theory, I was there by my own free will, but what else was I to do, really? Go back to a completely isolated situation at Bloor Street in this state? I don't know if I could technically have checked myself out at any point, but it certainly didn't seem to be a possibility. The door to the outside world had closed and all I was left with was faith—and I was beginning to wonder how much further I could get with that as my only fuel. I was now in another realm of ghosts and shadow: this one wasn't the ashes from the bonfire of excess but the residue of a hand dealt from a pack full of jokers.

The first few days were what you might imagine—sleepless nights due to roommates, medication changes, and the general atmosphere of despondence and extreme unpredictability. After that, some level of routine set in—even though I'm not quite certain that actually exists in such an environment. Whatever it was, it involved daily meetings with several doctors, various therapy and support groups, mindfulness and meditation sessions, several classes and groups (that might have approached kindergarten level), along with mandatory mealtimes three times a day. I believe there was also mandatory television-watching, since it seemed to take place several times a day—or maybe that was just me.

It was typical institutionalization, with the added benefit of permitting me to witness levels of insanity most will never be privy to—and that I was supposedly included in. Being in a facility for mental unwellness is both a horrifying ordeal and a powerfully enlightening one, as you observe others at their most vulnerable and weak, while at the same time, their most wild and out-of-control. I must have been somewhere on that spectrum, even though it didn't seem that way to me. But it probably never does.

After some time there, the rest of the "team" started to reappear in the form of personal support workers, case managers, lawyers, and the rest. I was obviously in no reasonable condition to deal with this most recent development, nor was I consulted about any of the choices of those there for my "benefit." I would assume they realized whatever they imagined they were doing didn't work and some other course of action had to be taken while I was still breathing (because if I wasn't, they of course wouldn't get paid). This led to more games on all sides, because the endgame still hadn't happened. It's difficult to say what the endgame of the psych ward was, especially since I wasn't particularly insane when I went in, but I would guess it revolved around having some reasonable capacity to deal with the upcoming circumstances, not following through on the threat to jump in Lake Ontario (even though, at times, that appeared to be a more pleasant ride). One of the requirements of such an establishment is to protect one from oneself—a notion I don't quite agree with.

The initial objective was to get me onto some appropriate medication. As I recall, I wasn't on any at the time—or perhaps I was on the wrong ones—or some combination of both possibilities. Whatever it was, the adjustment period led to further insanity on my part, and what my doctor described as "psychotic" behaviour. This must have been quite bad, since I was already in a mental hospital! This, of course, led to me taking anti-psychotics, which I rejected after a few days due to the rather unpleasant, zombie-like state they induced. This undoubtedly led to the first of quite a few debates/arguments with my main doctor, since it's not generally accepted to refuse any form of treatment while in hospital. But that particular "cure" seemed to me to be worse than the illness, and I wasn't willing to go another step back, even if it led to a thousand steps forward. And since I went a pretty far way back with that doctor, he agreed to discontinue the anti-psychotics. On some matter most likely surrounding the medication issue, I got into a debate with one of the assistant doctors, which resulted in his conclusion that "You don't become superman overnight"—to which my response was, "Why not?" Within that debate lies the crucial difference between science and other forms of treatment and consciousness. Who can truly predict the future? But that kind of talk in a psych ward will only keep you there forever!

The longer you stay, the more tolerable it becomes—and my situation there came to seem more of an unfolding drama than a prison. What I mean by this is that as time went on, though the circumstances were no less intense, the rewards of what I would witness on a daily basis became somewhat greater than the struggle. It really was all a struggle—but it was definitely not pointless or meaningless. I would imagine that's why people venture into that line of work—because one simply gets to routinely witness critical scenarios the rest of the world aren't privy to, as

I was at each location where I made a stop. However, this one was by far the most dramatic, enlightening, and indeed, at times, terrifying, due to its nature as a mental facility. So, there I was again, between a rock and a hard place, not knowing what lay around the next bend. I don't mean to say, by any means, that the days flew by or became "easy," but I suppose home is home, and by this point in my journey, through trial by fire, I had learned how to make home anywhere. I'm also not trying to convince you to do your best to be invited to such a destination, but to look for something of depth in every situation—which is most definitely easier said than done.

After a few weeks, a plan for discharge was being put together with the doctors, myself, and the new "team" that would involve me going back to my Bloor Street apartment—which was almost literally just down the road—under the supervision of these virtual strangers. When faced with this option, I went, once again, into extension mode, determined to stay longer. Perhaps that is the one game I did play—but it was for good reason, as I saw it as a way of continuing a reality I might never see again, and I was learning a tremendous amount. Because I was continuing to receive treatment, and as long as progress was being made, they agreed to let it continue for a while. I imagine this was quite the conundrum for the doctors, since they want everyone to get better and improve. My doctor explained to me once that the hospital was "not exactly a hotel"— which I, for the most part, agreed with. But my conundrum was that once I left I knew things would not necessarily be *worse*, but certainly shallower and more out of balance. So, I was essentially running a race backwards in an effort to stay away from the finish line.

You may be wondering where my family was in all of this by this point—and they did begin to arrive during this phase—but because this is a meditation on finding yourself through the unknown, this is why there hasn't been much mention of them. At this point, I should emphasize that since hindsight is always twenty-twenty, I'm probably making all this appear far simpler than it actually was. It has now been over seven years since I was at Mt. Sinai, and as with my stays elsewhere, too much time has since passed for me to provide more detail. It is vital to understand that every one of the stages was a trial unto itself, even if I no longer remember it all. What has remained with me, of each stage of my journey, is that I made it through.

One of the moments I do remember from this period included the woman dressed in head-to-toe Chanel who I noticed one evening at the nursing station: she seemed to be checking in for the weekend or just stopping by to let everyone know she was still alive. Imagine the surreality of being surrounded by those whose greatest challenge was perhaps changing their clothes once a week (one of my challenges, at the time) or remembering their own name (something I was fortunate enough not to have an issue with), then noticing someone stroll through the heavily secured doors as though they might be looking for directions to the Oscars... only to find out that they were a resident! That left me puzzled as to the possible circumstances surrounding this individual. They certainly appeared to be different from those of everyone else— me included. Then again, I had come from NRIO, an institution that cost in the region of fifty thousand dollars a month, as I later found out—and there had been another client there who, as far as I understood, was convinced he was the leader of the global elite and was controlling it all from his laptop in the hospital (or something to that effect). The main point is to not be deceived by appearances—that's often all they are.

Another moment was the time I got into a more heated debate with my doctor, which resulted in him letting me know, in no uncertain terms, that he was the one who made the rules. I was quite aware of that—nonetheless, I had no issue with challenging them when I saw fit, perhaps not following them at all sometimes. Unfortunately, the establishment was not a fan of such insurrection. The truth of it is that rules are typically for the benefit of those who wrote them, not those who have to play by them. And if I had the ability to be a blind follower, I probably wouldn't have been in that particular predicament of being in the psych ward—as I believe would also be true of my fellow wandering souls. All of this was taking place during the height of a polar vortex. This had the effect of making the rare and all-too-brief ventures outside even more challenging than what was constantly unfolding inside. It was one of the rarest weather spectacles, which made it an ideal counterpart to the very unusual events I was experiencing at the same time.

There were also all the unexpected guests who saw it as a good time to drop in—which I, at times, agreed with and others, did not. A good question would be how they found out I was there in the first place. I certainly wasn't in regular contact with the outside world. The news of my grandmother's passing was brought by one of these visitors. She was at quite an advanced age, but this was nonetheless a bit of a surprise, and most definitely a peculiar issue to navigate, because this particular hospital unit had to know where you were when you weren't there. I also had hardly any clothes to speak of, much less appropriate funeral attire—and attempting to explain to people who were still virtual strangers where to find these things in your home was not as straightforward as it might sound. This event added to the surreality of the time, since I was in a daily struggle for my sanity due to both my surroundings and the reasons I was there in the first place. But this had to be done, as there was not going to be a repeat of the ceremony I missed for my friend in Ottawa. Fool me once and it's on you, fool me twice…

Once all the details were sorted out, I made it there, and it was good and right to do so, in spite of the obligatory pleasantries (and those who showed up only then, who surely would not be heard from or seen again). However, the air of darkness hanging around that day and the one hanging perpetually around my actual residence led to more questions and doubts about the meaning of it all and where I was really headed.

Far I never too far from I so look for I and I with your far eye and never fear I. I and I.

What more can I say about a place I could never find enough words in a thousand lifetimes to begin to capture? I don't believe even the doctors' notes would begin to do that job, because the doctors left at night. All I can say is it is what it is, and it carried on being what it was. By that point I must have been there at least a month, and the plans for me leaving were in full swing, whether or not I agreed—and of course, by then, I definitely did not because by then I had gotten to know that place and the entire song and dance routine. My view was that I had achieved a skillful balance between the harsh and often sterile reality and the point at which it all transforms into some state-sponsored version of a commune, though with slightly less free will involved. I considered it to be an act of some skill, because most would be out the door the very second the papers were signed. But my issue was that I didn't know what was on the outside—and what you don't know is what you don't know.

If you know what you know but don't know what you don't know and the more you know, the less you know (but you really don't know what you know), that what you don't know is your room to grow, you'll probably end up in a psych ward! Overstaying your welcome in such establishments may lead to this manner of debate, so perhaps that should have been a sign it was time to hit the road. Taking up residence in one's head for too long is probably not the best course of action, so the time was drawing nigh once again.

What I do know is that it's time to wrap up this chapter. On that note, let me bring this episode of my life full circle by describing when the unit morphed into a temple. That was close to the point I discovered one of the PSWs had the useful talent of playing the piano, which became more useful upon the discovery of a piano in the unit, which they had no issue with him playing, while I accompanied him on guitar. We proceeded to do this for a private audience of two—or anyone else who happened to pass by and stay, (which, at times, were quite a few). We would do this for the absolute maximum amount of time allowed, each and every occasion. Perhaps this was karma in action, or a random twist of fate. You choose. These are the choices we make constantly, that shape our fate—or the shape of our faith, if you will. I saw it then as the light beginning to shine through the cracks, the bud sprouting in winter. This was perhaps the first mustard seed of this trip—so I went with it, at that point.

Around this time, I must have become adjusted to some new medication following a period of purgatory—being a lab rat, seeing if a med works. It must have—otherwise, I would still be there. I was just as in the dark about the standards required to allow you to leave as I was about the ones that gave cause to arrive. But whatever gave rise to my apparent normalcy, discharge plans were afoot. The idea was for me to go back to my Bloor Street apartment along with the new "supports" in place, in addition to maintaining contact with the hospital should any mishaps occur (such as stumbling into a mountain of cocaine and having it all mysteriously make its way up my nose). I was also expected to attend follow-up appointments, and outpatient therapy as soon as the next week.

My prison had become my temple. My punishment had become my nourishment. I have gone on to find this theme runs through absolutely all existence, though it is simply a matter of perception. At times it doesn't appear as such, but it is. You've heard the stories of reaching enlightenment behind bars, the epic upsets, the child prodigy, the million-to-one shot, the last dollar spent on the winning lottery ticket, and your very own birth. In short, it's up to you. Get to it. Life is waiting—just take one step.

Perhaps when you get to the end of anything, the rose-coloured shades become your choice travel attire—but I've never had a pair, and don't know that I've seen any. And there are actually many shades of roses—including black (I've heard, but not seen). Nevertheless, I was at that point as I packed the bags—or bag, most likely, at that point, just enough to contain my now ill-fitting suit for my grandmother's funeral. I knew this had to be, and also had some idea what was to be, which wouldn't be this...

CHAPTER 10

Round Three

"Many of life's failures are people who did not realize how close they were to success before they gave up." – Thomas Edison

Wallet, keys, hit the breeze, leavin' the day to the trees, changin' like the leaves, but we're not gonna fall and we're not gonna leave, just like the trees, we've been here before, so just rise through it all, straight through the winter, then, springin' up like you've been here and back—don't turn your back. Keep bloomin', it's comin'...

So, where do we go from here? To the next stop, of course. This happened to be a return visit to 341 Bloor Street West. This was still the address where I received mail, though I hadn't actually resided there for close to a year. It had been the site of much destruction and mayhem as I have detailed earlier. Not much had changed at the building itself, but apparently I had—which tends to be the case after inhabiting three consecutive institutions for a period in the region of eighteen months.

The first major step was being in this dwelling while completely sober—which of course was far from the case before. Part of the program at Bellwoods was revisiting the place of major abuse for a brief time. I stopped by a few times to complete necessary domestic tasks—but these had amounted to a total of only a few hours, so this really was the first true test of my sobriety. It was a quick pass, as the cravings and memories did come, but just as surely left—which is the trick to the whole thing, really. The twelve-step work was giving evidence of cause and effect in full effect.

Despite that victory, there was the outside world to deal with. And that hadn't changed at all. All the temptations were still readily available. But the temptations remained just that due to the work, though it was nonetheless quite trying to witness the scenes I had once been in. Still, I wasn't willing to pay the high price of low quality when it comes to chasing thrills.

We were getting to the final stages of my legal drama, and though I wasn't aware of it at the time, they were about to prepare for the pressure defence. What I'm saying here is that it was getting close to the five-year point since my case had begun—which was the new estimation point for it to go to settlement. At a meeting with my lawyer shortly after my discharge from the hospital, I was informed this indeed seemed to be the case. I'm not certain I ever actually said "put me in, coach" or "I'm taking the shot." But that's the play that was called, so it was preordained for me to go through a test of life in order to be granted a chance at a new one. What can I say? Life isn't cheap, and neither is justice. My original lawyer once said, "Pain and suffering is pain and suffering." Those words were now turning out to be all too prophetic.

The chase was on for the finish line of my legal case. Discussions regarding the date of the settlement day must have surely begun by then, as both sides only have so long they can remain on the fence. I had jumped off for some time, but the insurance side was still doing a balancing act, the usual games. Well, my lawyer explained that the monitoring, surveillance, "supports" and all the rest of it were increasing—to an amount I said was unacceptable. This twilight zone that had become my reality, even in my own dwelling, was already far past the point any reasonable human would deem reasonable. His response was that there was no choice but to continue. If not, we would run the risk of forfeiting the entire case—which was definitely not in his or my interests after having come this far. He didn't say it in as many words, but it was clear to me that their game was now to do everything within their power to break me—but I was in for the long game. *Go ahead, do your worst*, I pondered on the way back from that meeting. This was never between me and them—this was between me and creation itself. They would have to kill me to put me on the sidelines at that point. Perhaps an actual shot from a gun would have been a more pleasant. Now, I'm not speaking badly of the individuals that were put in place to play out these schemes. They were, after all, through no fault of their own, pawns in a game. But as they were the actual, physical manifestations of the ones on the other side of the fence, they did have to deal with the majority of my wrath. It could not be directed at the appropriate targets, who always hid behind closed doors and walls of paper. I was certainly more than somewhat unreasonable with them at times, but unlike me, they had known what they had signed up for when accepting these positions. To them, it was a mere job, while it was *life* to me.

While still at Mt. Sinai, a daily routine of activities with the two new PSWs had already begun—I imagine as some sort of test or preparation for what was to come. Well, here it was, and I had no say in it. Firstly, having two individuals for this task was completely excessive, even though they were there, for the most part, at separate times. Similar to when I was with NRIO, I was accompanied to virtually all engagements other than using the toilet. That is barely an exaggeration. This time, however, just to keep things interesting—and, in my estimation, to test my limits just a bit further—once I moved back to Bloor St., one of them was also stationed while I was at home to do God knows what, with the additional plot twist that this was a tiny bachelor apartment known to be my former central location for drug abuse. Let me remind you that this whole arrangement was, in theory, there to *protect* and ensure my sobriety.

This was to me a personal affront, even though on some level, I really did know it was the work of some demented puppet-master somewhere in the ether. When someone claims to be there for your benefit, but the evidence shows you've both accomplished nothing more than staring at the walls for the past few hours, turning the other cheek becomes an Olympic act—which, more often than not, I was unable to complete. I wasn't privy to what these individuals were getting paid, even though I was the one paying it, but I would conclude that they were questioning their choices just as much as I was. With the lack of space, dealing with the same two people everyday was a situation literally too close for comfort. The result was some level of conflict on an almost-daily basis—largely dependent on what type of activity I was involved in with them. But when stuck in solitary confinement with one of them, it was always an issue. It is a miracle beyond compare it remained only a test of wills rather than fists.

Faced again with being stuck between a rock and an ever increasingly hard place, the only progressive option was to make friends with the rock, the hard place, and both people. I'm not implying these individuals were evil or had bad intentions, but I had to find some common ground with them to make any level of existence possible. This seemed to work to some degree, and there were moments of levity, along with obligatory affirmations of camaraderie that may or may not have been true. What is true is that I have had little contact with either of them since the job ended. I must say, though, that one of them was one of the more humane examples I encountered on this odyssey, and I have his phone number to this day. Even though there is no practical reason for him to answer my calls, he still does.

The light was shining through the cracks—even though I only had one eye open then.

The goal of what I have to say now is not to expose people but to expose you to truths in yourself, I hope, that may have been hidden and to the truths of my struggle that provides evidence of the miracle I continue to tell. In that vein, I must use my artistic license as justification for what I am about to illustrate. As I have mentioned, a team was put together around me to supposedly protect me from myself and assist in implementing habits I might have lost due to my injuries. It would be of benefit to my general progress as time and life carried on after their services were no longer available. I believe this process began without my knowledge or input close to the end of my time at Bellwoods. As far as I understand it, these individuals were chosen by my case manager at the time.

The relationship between this woman and me had been reasonable enough up to that point considering the circumstances, which is why I would imagine she went ahead with the choices. Or perhaps there were pressures from the other side, which would be my suspicion, though I cannot say for certain. What I definitely can say is that the person who was chosen, in theory to supervise the support workers, turned out to be one of the most heinous individuals I have been unfortunate enough to ever cross paths with. He was a thief because he took money for helping me but he never did anything to help—all he did was harm me with his empty promises and lack of caring. I will call him the devil. This judgement is a result of the evidence of him not completing a single task one would imagine to be required of someone in such a position.

As an example, on two occasions he took me to locations where he assured me he knew people in positions that would allow them to hire me as long as I showed up and told them my qualifications and filled out an application. On both occasions, I asked him whether he was absolutely certain, and on both occasions, he looked at me and boldly proclaimed there was no doubt. At that time, I was still a trusting person who didn't automatically assume the worst of people—an ability I am still working on regaining. But what I am boldly proclaiming here is that absolutely nothing resulted from both these situations, and when I would ask about them, he would respond as if he had no idea what I was talking about. Keep in mind this person was entrusted to oversee major aspects of the progress and health of a person with injuries deemed by the highest of authorities to be catastrophic in nature. This is only a brief example of an endless list of offences by this person in what I consider to be a case of neglect and corruption.

Another example is that during the time of his tenure, which I would estimate to be at least a year, he showed up at my place of residence precisely twice, only at the very beginning and—you guessed it—the very end. I have often wondered how these types live with themselves, and what I have come to realize is that they *don't*. I have also come to understand the only way it becomes so easy to lie to others is if you've been doing so to yourself far longer. On the last occasion of his appearance, which was a time at when I could barely stand on my feet, he made some twisted threat in the costume of yet another promise. I was in such mental state at the time that I could not totally comprehend what he had actually said—which turned out to be a fortunate thing for him and me both.

He had presented himself in a respectable manner, because a thief always needs a good disguise, and he must have been quite experienced in appearing to be a stranger to himself for years. I sincerely hope he comes across these words one day, with the knowledge that it has taken me years to get past this hate. I used to wonder how such types sleep at night but I realize now they probably don't, due to the race they're running against ghosts and shadows. I hope karma has caught up with him without too much damage being caused. If it hasn't, it surely will. No one escapes... you can't outrun yourself.

What I can thank him and his possible cohorts for is that witnessing such stark darkness and illusion gave me the ability to witness the light and truth in myself and others much more rapidly. I went on to discover he—and I use that term loosely—was being compensated quite handsomely the entire time he was involved in my case. This sad truth was no surprise, though, because these types require layers of adornment to cover up their shame and guilt, like the addict who, after crossing the line, will do just about anything to avoid withdrawal and face themselves naked—a situation I didn't quite get to, but close enough. There is no conscience left when it comes to getting that fix, and in my situation, I am certain it was nothing but a means to some ends only he knew. I used to imagine what might have happened if we crossed paths unexpectedly, alongside keeping score, counting my days for revenge. Now, however, I know I would carry on my way, letting out a huge laugh he would have no choice but to hear, with the knowledge that something *is* keeping score—but it's not me.

Unfortunately, he was not the only one who professed to be there to help me, but who didn't. One of the cleverer ones was another woman, my original case manager, who did absolutely nothing toward the benefit of my progress back when I had my original lawyer—before going to Bellwoods, as best I can recall—but managed to show up at my apartment right before my settlement date at court, for most likely the one and only time, at literally the last moment required for her to get something signed by me to ensure she got paid before I left the residence for an extended period. It was also just in time for me to see her speed away in her shiny BMW.

That goes back to my point about costumes, since up to that point, she had given the appearance of nothing but simplicity and humility. I was able to fire her with absolutely no regret, but her replacement was another story. I may as well tell you that story.

The next case manager, did do an admirable job in the beginning in initiating some progress her predecessor was either unwilling or unable to accomplish. Again, the details escape me now and they don't affect the overall point I'm getting at, but suffice it to say, she fulfilled the expectations of her title. This particular individual's surname was an exact match to her choice appearance and has also turned out to be an exact match to the theory I mentioned on costumes and disguises. The only complaint I could have made about her up until her choice of support workers and their superior was her being too friendly and positive.

Looking back on it now, I'm quite certain it was a premeditated plot on their parts. I can't prove any of this, but what I can attest to is that she was another who swore up and down it wasn't all about the bottom line, that my well-being and future were priorities, that she would ensure people were in place once the settlement happened so that my life could too, that she would carry on in her role—basically, that there was a long-term plan in place. Those were all nice words, but what wasn't, was that the minute my case settled, she disappeared like all the rest.

During this phase, the number of tangible tests I was made to do also increased drastically, along with apparent surveillance, in addition to being questioned at length on all variety of topics related to my general capacities. By the way, they already knew the answers to all these questions, because all of this had been done previously—and my injuries were no secret to anyone involved. I can't say for certain it was at exactly the same time, but there was also an increase in my visits to doctors on the other side for what amounted to interrogations about what had already been known for quite some time. In their estimation, I suppose it could be possible to fake a catastrophic accident five years after the fact. I also had absolutely no doubt surveillance had been taking place prior to these events. They would certainly disagree with this, including that the surveillance was increased in the final phase, but take it from me, since I really don't have much to gain at this point (other than telling the truth so others may be aware).

Beyond all that, I'm certain there were even more unexpected plot twists my memory has conveniently displaced but I'm sure you get the picture by now. In the midst of all this there was still progress in what

I would call my *real* life—even though all the lines were blurred to the point of appearing to be circles by then. That glimmer of hope came in the form of being accepted to be a peer mentor volunteer for drug addiction back at Bellwoods. This provided me an oasis in the desert the rest of existence was becoming through no fault of my own other than seeking justice and a sustainable future. The position consisted primarily of telling my story of addiction to the clients—one in the not-so-distant past, though it now felt like another lifetime. Looking in the rearview mirror, I can now see how vital sobriety was in providing me the tools to navigate the avalanche that swept over me the minute I left those doors.

The clients at Bellwoods were genuinely appreciative of what I had to offer, and I went religiously in the beginning, in part for the incredible respite from all the talk of my finances (as there was not a mention of that). So, once again, the limbo sessions were in full effect, with the days at Bellwoods at one end of the seesaw and everything else firmly rooted on the other. This must have been around the summer of 2015, as I recall volunteering at a few outdoor events. The routine carried on for another few months, until it didn't. It seems a soul has its limit, and mine arrived somewhere before the depths of winter. For the most part, I simply stopped. Stopped dealing with the bullshit, stopped going to appointments, stopped answering the phone, stopped going outside, stopped taking the blame for what I didn't do, stopped going to the grocery store, and even stopped going to Bellwoods. Just about the only things that didn't stop was life itself—and keeping an eye on the finish line even while they were closed.

What can be said about the final chapter of this chapter? Not a hell of a lot, but I'm going to anyway, since that appears to be what I do these days. The open-eyed winter slumber party of 2014—my temporary transformation into a hibernating bear—began innocently enough, as most significant undertakings tend to. In this peculiar tale of hiding in plain sight, the genesis was discovering completely accidentally that it was possible to reasonably pass an entire weekend without leaving my apartment or even my bed. I had been playing a bit of a cat-and-mouse game on the weekends with the opposite side, insisting I wasn't home in order to avoid the complications of the typical weekdays, after no small amount of negation had gained me the "privilege" of not having to be monitored every weekend. But they still persisted in checking in every now and then—or there would actually be something scheduled. They all still appeared to be convinced that I was in some sort of danger with them not around. Whatever their game was, my weekend game didn't involve them in any way, shape, or form—which became another burden in itself. After a few rounds of this, one weekend, I just said I wasn't available—even though I was and had no plans of my own. So, I had trapped myself even further. Up until then, I would always find some activities outside to do—in large part, due to the assumption that staying inside for any extended period would become so unpleasant as to not be recommended. However, because I'd done absolutely nothing that required any amount of energy, Monday morning arrived and I was no worse for wear—other than perhaps having regressed slightly as a human being. On paper, it must have been a result of my complete exhaustion from the games, but at the time, it appeared to me as some miraculous door opening into a world of complete withdrawal—what others might call avoidance. You may be asking what I'm really going on about here, other than a simple weekend of sloth. But I had never seen this as a possible route out of the dense forest I was venturing ever further into. Life often creates a way out of no way, if you are only willing to take it.

So began yet another routine... but this was to be the routine of no routine, if you can conceive of that. If it didn't involve some aspect of slothdom and possible personal decay, it didn't involve me. Mercifully and miraculously, substance abuse of any kind were not ingredients in the slowly simmering soup of indifference. This turn of events was in no way pleasurable or even indulgent—even though it may appear so. The most expected perception would be that I was simply waiting for the cheque to arrive. I can assure you this phase was not organized by me. The wave of gradual withdrawal simply washed over, without me having much say in it, quite quickly—much like a drug addiction. There was the similar sense that once you wake up to your circumstances, it's too late, since you're already there. This time, when I made my bed, I was literally lying in it. But actually making the bed was far too advanced an undertaking to consider at that juncture. The more mysterious element here was that I was somehow fine with the nature of the proceedings—and they did actually solve a problem, whereas drugs only provided the illusion of doing so (while actually causing far greater ones).

Without exaggeration, the entire winter passed without me going out for more than a maximum of four days—and those were only to do activities absolutely essential to existence. The support workers and the rest would probably say that they were responsible for keeping me breathing during that time, but would conveniently neglect to mention them putting me in that position in the first place. It still perplexes me that you could get into such a state with an army of doctors and others purporting to be there for your benefit. It remains miraculous to me that I came out of all that somewhat intact, since being completely inactive for such a length of time should have had a much more serious effect, as I understand it. To this day, I am quite certain the forces of karma took over and allowed me to go into a kind of human hibernation and still be able to wake up. If I had been guilty of any of what the accusations and lies said of me, I doubt I would be here today—and I would definitely not have been able to survive the onslaught that carried on until the very last hurdle. That last hurdle was now firmly in sight as my settlement meeting had at last been scheduled.

I hope this paints a picture of what that time was like, because it certainly was quite trying to even revisit here. Perhaps you can imagine actually living it—even though "living" might not be the most accurate description of that passage of time. Not much else happened other than others' concern increasing—especially my mother. But I obviously didn't share them. As time went on, I continued to skip medical appointments of all types, along with anything else that might have been deemed valuable in my situation. There wasn't much anyone could really say or do about this course of action (again, much like with an addiction). When you're done, you're done, and no one can make you listen.

"If you haven't confidence in self, you are twice defeated
in the race of life. With confidence, you have won
even before you have started." - Marcus Garvey

I'll leave you to ponder, for a moment, how that statement could possibly apply to doing virtually nothing for the better part of an entire season. Hopefully, by the time we get to the end of it all, it will make perfect sense. One of my primary attempts in this work is to get you to know yourself in such a way that you cannot be moved in any direction without your permission. Many ages ago, I heard Bob Marley speaking about the difference between knowing and believing, which wasn't quite clear to me until I had faced many trials in my life. One of my efforts here is to spare you that travel time.

I somehow knew I would cross the finish line, despite all appearances, as the final steep climb arrived. I'm certain most of those around me had doubts whether I would even make it out of bed that day, and if not, what they would have to do to ensure I got there (in however many pieces). I did not share these concerns. I *knew*—as opposed to hoped—that the same force that had gotten me this far would do what was required for the rest of the way home.

We've got a mighty long way to travel and we've got a mighty long way to go. We've got a mighty long way to travel, but we're on the way home. We've got a mighty long way to travel and a mighty long way to go. We've got a mighty long way to travel, but we're not walking alone.

I was in just about the worst possible condition to be heading to an event of such magnitude. The only riskier condition I can conceive of would be complete intoxication on powerful narcotics. I held strong to the opinion that my feelings of absolute indifference and isolation were by no means an accident but a thoroughly calculated ploy by the other side to break me before it was time to render onto Caesar. But what do I know? I only had front-row centre season tickets for the duration of the games. It may not be to my benefit to maintain this stance, but it wouldn't be to *not* do so either, so there you have it. The truth is what I stand on, and what has allowed me to stand, and it will remain so.

At some other point along the road, a stone turned up that said things tend to end the same way they begin—and that rang true in this case. I was in just as much of a fog as I had been when the suits first showed up and the games began. Now that the heavy lifting had been done and the finish line was in clear view, it was much like it was when I first woke up after being left by the side of the road. The only difference was that the current catastrophe had been brought on by blows to my consciousness as opposed to spine and brain—and it took approximately five years for all the symptoms to show.

A few days before my settlement meeting, the devil made his one and only appearance at my "home," with his lackeys in tow, as some sort of ludicrous show of force—as those who possess no power are wont to do. It seemed his visit was meant to be threatening, something I found preposterous and hilarious. It's been a long time, now, but I recall this to have been done to convince me that I had to show up to the hearing for my benefit, and that they would still be around to assist me, no matter what the outcome was. It may also have been to persuade me to keep them employed—which would also, of course, be "for my own good." It didn't escape me what a shallow and thinly veiled attempt at honour and dignity this last-minute farce was. The whole thing made me even more sick, despite the fact that the devil had long since shown his hand. I suppose I still had some faint hope of humanity on his part. My message with this is that people are what they are, even if they aren't aware of it, and I would much rather you shoot me in the face than the back. I don't know what exactly he and his cohorts expected to come of their empty words, since I had already shown my cards long ago, but all it resulted in was further contempt in me for the entire house of cards that was about to fall. Hindsight has gone on to show me that these types never change unless forced to, and even then, it may not last. But I leave that up to the forces of karmic judgement, with my current goal being to let the inmates run the asylum while I carry on carrying on. As for the situation at hand, it might be useful to mention that unlike the original coma five years before, this time around, it was for the most part self-induced—and roughly twenty times longer!

CHAPTER 11

Judgement Day

My day arrived one early and appropriately bleak late winter morning, with just a bit more torture in order. I sized up my options that morning and arose from my hibernation. I was now on the hunt: Judgement Day was now upon me—or justice day. At least, justice in the form it is currently practised—at least, what was available to me then. In other words, settlement day. It only took five and a half years to manifest, which had almost taken my life again in the process. But here it was—and here it is, in all its finery. I still don't know how to do the math on a life drastically altered or that there is an accurate equation for such a phenomenon, but there we were.

And what else was I going to do at that point, really? This was what I had signed up for. In our current version of society, which I'm still at odds with, actually, it is acceptable or even expected that one receive money as recompense for pain and suffering, if at all possible. Perhaps we think retail therapy will fix everything. I had my own ideas of what would be an appropriate value for that transaction, but to tell the truth, the best deal would be that the chapter would finally be signed, sealed, and delivered, allowing me to live life in real time once again. This was a day unlike all the rest. It meant all the rest were to come—quite literally.

My initial victory was simply making it to the downtown location, which was in an area where such matters were typically conducted. It was on Bay Street, to be precise, which is somewhat ironic, since it is a section of town where sunlight can barely get through all the buildings, yet this day was designed to take me out of the dark. But this was a day of practicalities rather than musings—there had already been more than five years of that. All the expected parties where there. Namely, lawyers from both sides, insurance representatives of all kinds, and my humble mother—who was essentially representing me, due to my questionable state. She wasn't equipped to negotiate on my behalf, but neither was I, so she did what she could. I recall there being some type of mediator also present, in addition to other sorts of characters in dark suits you might expect at such a gathering.

As far as my expectations or hopes for the day were concerned, I was seeking to be compensated to the tune of the numbers I had been discussing with my lawyers from the very start. I held no delusions this would be like a winning lottery ticket, which would allow me to indulge in all manner of pleasures for the rest of time, though I did have good reason to believe I would be remunerated for the loss of a lifetime's worth of reasonable employment opportunities—not to mention the loss of capacity to participate in typical society and what most would consider to be normal living. I should mention, at this point, the particulars that made any amount of compensation feasible in the first place. It goes roughly as follows. As we know, I was hit off a bicycle on June 4, 2010 and left on the road. What I later learned was that the driver was subsequently charged with a hit-and-run leading to the injuries I have described here—and perhaps even more. This driver was arrested at some point not too long after that, in the rented vehicle he had been driving at the time of the incident. The rental company is the one the suit was then brought against, which allowed for the possibility of some reasonable compensation.

All the players in the game were there, and the cards were all on the table, so I suppose that what was left to do was count the chips and split them up appropriately. I don't specifically recall the numbers negotiated, but as I've found to be typical in such procedures, it ended up somewhere close to the middle. I'm certain my team asked for the stars, and the insurance side responded with the moon, and it all landed closer to Earth. I observed it all with a slight detachment, still. I was barely there, still, to tell the truth—which was actually ideal for my role since even if I had been wide awake, there wouldn't have been much of an effect on the proceedings. The cards had already been dealt, so my less-than-optimum state might have turned out to be an ace in the hole as evidence of the cumulative effects of the incident—unless, of course, their joker was that I had been faking it the whole time.

I don't know what they went all day from room to room discussing, but I was left to peruse the surroundings—which were quite luxurious, laden with distraction and nourishment—which I would imagine was a concerted effort to take one's focus off the significance of the realities of the day. Or perhaps this particular species of shark required vast amounts of energy to swim in this extended body of water.

One curious outcome early in the day was the financial consequence of my time of excess and madness with the result being something that I can tell you definitely wasn't worth it on any level other than being able to tell the tale now. All my recovery had been financed through loans against my settlement but I was never aware of the amount. The particular discovery that the amount totaled some $80,000 was quite shocking, and the consideration of what this money could have been used for other than constructing a tunnel to Colombia in my nose, required absolutely all the therapy and study I had undertaken up to that point to let go of.

It was a dramatic day, a microcosm of the previous five years, in that I had to drop all attachment and expectation at each and every stop in favour of trusting I had done my part to the utmost of my abilities and honour, and recognize the result as out of my hands (though with the hope that a few chips would fall in my direction). I've relentlessly echoed here how that perspective has been a vital tool in getting me to this point, borne of the events I've described thus far. I continue to hope what I've captured here will prove to be less treacherous an odyssey for you to traverse than mine was in order to locate these pearls. Basically, I hope this will be a catalyst for you to discover the treasures waiting for you.

The day carried on. They would arrive at the conclusion of a certain part of the case and move on to the next. The process ultimately involved all that had already taken place, and the rest would be arrived at based off my reasonable life expectancy, which was calculated to be in the region of sixty-five years or more. I would be lying if I said I wouldn't have voted for the higher numbers on my side of the ledger while watching from the sidelines, yet my overall purpose was to close this door with a deadbolt. But putting a cherry on top is always a nice touch.

As far as I was concerned, I deserved the fiscal possibility of charting a new course, since whichever one I had been on before had encountered the mother of all storms. The possibility of putting a few more zeroes to my name was also enticing. I knew that on its own, a more impressive bank account would not a new life make, but it would allow me to partake of and participate in life on a different level, playing a new role that would enhance the skills required to be deattached from any one role or identity. In other words, once you've sampled everything the table has to offer, you can really make your selection. When you consider that I had been sampling reheated leftovers for quite some time, it seemed prudent to step up to the plate and order the catch of the day. I was headed a bit further down the rabbit hole. This journey had separated me from almost everything I'd ever known, so why not keep going in the same direction, toward Neverneverland? Remember that you can't keep any of it other than the stories.

Finally, I had reached the other side of the day, where most of the i's had been dotted and t's crossed. The results, which I wasn't privy to that day, seemed to be reasonable enough based on the responses of my family and legal team. As far as what was immediately disclosed, it was satisfactory for the most part, putting good value on my struggle and meeting some of my personal criteria. I would not say, however, that I hit the jackpot by any means—which tends to be a common misconception by those peering in from beyond the fences—but rather, that it provided for that decent chance at a restart and possibly a good therapeutic break or two before that and as time went on. I can tell you that my formula for calculating a life's value would've rounded out to a slightly higher number, with the logic being that if a good majority of one's options were negated or drastically altered, it would stand to reason that an effort toward justice would provide for the compensation of those options in equal parts. For that to be the case, I would argue that one would have to be put into such a position that all of life's necessities are provided for, along with the resources necessary to pursue many avenues should it take time to reach a new, sustainable reality.

Coming up with an appropriate number was made more complex because the necessities of this particular life had increased in cost drastically—for reasons I trust have been made obvious. Without venturing into the ugliness of numbers, let's just say that my estimation would have been a few degrees north of what was arrived at—but perhaps that's why my qualifications are in survival and stubbornness as opposed to the legal arena. The other tangible hindrance that resulted in keeping my numbers south of the border was that, according to what was on paper, I barely existed prior to June 4, 2010 in terms of employment or taxes, so there was no way to logically assess what my financial future was likely to have been. If I had just completed a dental degree or had been selling cars for five years, for example, I would be writing this in January from a location a bit further south than Toronto. It would seem my lawyers had returned to the smoke-and-mirrors act to secure what they did for me, since that's what they were working with when it came to the feasibility of my past.

What can I say other than that karma will certainly take a significant bite out of the other side's ass. They had been performing the same act continuously for the better part of five years. You might say, at the end of it all, I was compensated at a level that might have been expected of someone who had just completed five years' rigorous study in a highly specialized field (without then having the responsibility of actually showing up to work). It just so happened I was the only one accepted into the program—and therefore, was the only graduate. This is probably good—I don't believe too many would have shown up to the final exam, and it's virtually unheard of to find an occupation in your field after you've received the diploma! I hope you can grasp the humour and levity I'm employing at this point, since I've come to accept that you (or perhaps *I*) have to laugh it all off at some point—and that point is now.

All kidding aside, it turned out to be one for the books. Even though all was not revealed that day, it was enough to know I could book my ticket to a new identity—not just practically, but more importantly (or maybe equally as importantly), mentally—as it brought the possibility of emerging from the shadows of the drama of the games into the sunshine of living for the day, in every sense. The knowledge and confidence I gained from staying the course remains today, and it is a far greater treasure than the money, but I can tell you I didn't turn it down. Balance in all things is required to truly evolve. I can also say that having made it to the finish line of the games—even though I virtually crawled over the line—I no longer involve myself in that type of activity. No, sir—no more games for me, other than the one I was born into. So, what you see is what you get, my friend. Take it or leave it. But more importantly, take *yourself*—because that's always with you.

The waiting game did, for the most part, work out for me in the (really) long run—but unless you find yourself being dealt such a rare hand, I wouldn't recommend it. Plot your course and see it through, but be open to the mystery, too. That is there every day, like the birds that sing for you. I'm going to go ahead and put some points on the board for myself for making it through to the other side. As should you, if you've been able to make sense of this dribble so far!

I came, I saw, I conquered... at least for a day.

CHAPTER 12

Exile on Yonge Street

It's the same grass on the other side—otherwise, you couldn't see it.

So I guess you thought it was over? Oh, how I wished it had been! But I've also heard that a dream without a plan is a wish—and apparently, it is prudent to plan your work and work your plan. All that aside, the unfortunate truth was that, on some critical levels, this saga was just beginning. The Hollywood version would say that when one door closes, another one opens, but my version says that when one door opened, the entire building got boarded up. On paper, the pages would seem to have been turning—but that stack of paper turned out to be most useful as kindling. What do I mean? My circumstances directly following settlement day appeared to be ideal. No more burden of proof, no reason to hide, no more "support" workers to nimbly avoid—but all of that was also the issue, since what you know is what you know, and what you don't is what you don't.

I now had what some might refer to as financial freedom, but freedom is only freedom if you know what to do with it—otherwise, you're quite free to be dumb. The world was telling me this was the time to take off, but due to the toll of the previous five years, I was firmly grounded. All the material pieces were now in place, but once all the final loose ends had been tied up and I had relocated from Bloor Street uptown, to the hinterland of Yonge and Finch, I found myself unable to move those pieces to their strategically appropriate locations on the chessboard. You could liken the situation to having a brand-new car, then finding the engine won't start. Since time is no longer our ally, I'm just going to give you a general outline of how this phase played itself out.

After even further trials and tribulations, I managed, with considerable assistance and encouragement, to get it together to a point at which I was able to make a move from Bloor Street roughly about a month or so following the settlement (since I apparently was as yet unsettled). It also appeared, at the time, that the unknown might carry more weight than the known, since the argument all around me was that virtually anyone would have immediately jumped at the chance to leave that epic disaster in the dust. But by now, you can surely see that I'm lots of things, but typical was never one. And you can't jump too far with half a spine!

I imagine there were logical reasons for my hesitation, but eventually, I went through the whole fake estate runaround—and yes, I said fake—and found a condominium at Yonge and Finch, which seemed to be in accordance with my circumstances at the time. It was still winter, then, which put even more pressure on finding living arrangements but generally, something had to be done, since I was no longer of a status to be in a subsidized building. The whole buying process further unsettled me with being unfamiliar with it and still not being fully awake to tell the truth. Nonetheless, the deal went down, and when it was done, it was done—even though up to the very last moments, there was hesitation on my part, partly due to the fact it was the most significant of my life by far at that time—in addition to it not being the dream destination by any stretch of the imagination. If you're familiar with Toronto, you'll know what I mean when I call it a no-man's (or anyone else's, for that matter) land. That part of town is neither here nor there in terms of character or culture, but the price was right, and it would be out of the downtown core. Perhaps the whole thing was ill-fated from the start, but that's the benefit of hindsight again. Something had to happen, and purchasing this condo appeared to be the most progressive of courses—and a good enough location to park some capital and plot out the future. The hope was that I would begin anew there and move from strength to strength.

Unfortunately, things went sideways once again, and the knowledge gained this time was that wherever you go, truly, there you are. My mere change of physical location did not have the intended effect of catalyzing me toward general progress. In fact, it had the opposite effect. After relocating, which had none of the typical sense of victory of one's first foray into home ownership, I sunk, rapidly, deeper into the quicksand. The main reason for this was that all my "team" members had now vanished other than the one respectable individual—but even he had no success with their repeated attempts at motivation. Everyone around tried, but I was firmly stuck in place once again, with the only difference being that this time, there was a far better view—which gave me more reason to stare at it for days and weeks on end.

As difficult as they had been, the immediately preceding circumstances had been essentially my entire existence—my daily structure and routine for several years. It had all disappeared like a puff of smoke, save for a few people who were straightforward with me from the very start. As a result of all that, being left to my own devices after that prolonged period of enforced support, I now found myself increasingly unable, or unwilling, or a combination of both, to complete or, at times, even attempt the majority of the routine activities of daily living, such as hygiene, paying bills, buying food, getting dressed, answering the phone—or even turning it on, for that matter. In theory, all these tasks should have been way easier, now, with all the other pressures taken off. Or I could have easily employed someone else to do them—but that didn't seem like a viable option, either.

What did turn out to be an option, then? Well, sleeping, blocked toilets, not leaving the house, tears, blame, regret, fear, never turning the stove on, getting to know the Chinese food delivery man far too well, and all other things you may associate with the return of sloth and indifference. This was another runaway train, and it kept spiraling off the tracks into ever lower realms of darkness and confusion. I must again emphasize I took no pleasure in any of this, as it might otherwise now appear I was simply an entitled asshole who refused to take the first step in a new direction. It would make complete sense for you to have such an opinion of me in this circumstance. I know that many who were aware of what I was doing (or not doing) did have this opinion of me because I was in quite an ideal setup on paper—if I could only have gotten the damn thing out of park.

No one really noticed my slothful ways for a while, in part because there was no one really around. And perhaps I didn't really notice it—or maybe I didn't see it as much of an issue, since I wasn't seeing anything clearly at the time. I definitely cannot recall what my daily routine was to any degree other than that my existence now was possibly an even more interminable struggle than it had just been previously—which may be as difficult for you to comprehend as it was for me then. Of course, the longer I couldn't or wouldn't accept it, the longer it went on.

And on it went—though heading nowhere, really, other than the further depths of my own consciousness—which I got lost in on several occasions, and barely made it back out the other side. Again, you can't make this stuff up—even though I surely wish I were, because even dredging this back up now is no joyride. But I must maintain my stance, to bring you the truth as it was. Otherwise, it was all for naught.

There were a few emergency calls from the building for what specific reasons, I'm not sure, along with the ones made by my mother—which resulted in some form of medical emergency workers knocking on my door to make sure I was fine. I wasn't, but I explained it away, because I quite simply didn't wish to deal with it. Over the course of months, this would happen again, occasionally, but what was I going to do? Voluntarily check myself into some institution for the umpteenth time, when I was now supposed to actually have a life? No sir, no thanks.

I *really* didn't sign up for the fight this time. The only fight I had left was to know, somehow, that I couldn't punch my own ticket to the next dimension. That was the one and only thing that kept me here when I was lost in the clouds on those long nights.

Somewhere within this mess, I discovered I had been carrying on for the previous five and a half years with an untreated brain injury as a result of the accident, which all the doctors had somehow either missed or avoided, for whatever reason. I was now on a wait list for a facility that specialized in whatever it was I had. At the time, I could not say whether the news of that was met by me with much hope or further indifference, but some of the information did provide some reasons as to why I was where I was. Another fucking waiting game? Hadn't one just ended?

CHAPTER 13

Words Aren't Enough

"No matter how hard the waves are, you will
float on the ocean." – Kubra Sait

One day, I had an appointment at the family doctor, which I debated attending for days. For some reason I did, most likely because it was one of the few engagements I was still maintaining over the course of yet another lost winter. The result of the appointment would prove to be the end of this chapter. I probably didn't have a specific reason for the appointment other than to have some human contact that didn't require me to participate in a particularly respectable condition. And they would have some comprehension of my present state of dysfunction. The doctor asked a few questions and took a few looks at me and determined that I would not be allowed to leave unless I was headed to CAMH, otherwise known as the Centre for Addiction and Mental Health, the budget-level psychiatry ward in Toronto, if you don't mind me saying. I'm qualified to—I've been in more than my fair share.

Simply put, this is not somewhere one wants to be. Mt. Sinai and all the rest were the Ritz compared to what this stop would turn out to be. I don't specifically know why I proceeded there from the doctor's office, as I technically didn't have to, and I had no police escort. But it seemed I really did have to, and unless I pulled the plug that night, the family doctor would have gotten word soon enough, and an escort would certainly have been at my door not long thereafter. When I got there the obligatory questioning session began. I wasn't certain whether I was attempting to talk my way in or out at that point. That confusion alone was probably grounds for being admitted, but the discussion carried on for some amount of time, until the inevitable happened. It was determined CAMH would be the best option as my new temporary residence. I had a reasonable notion of what I was in for, even though this was by no means the way I had pictured my day ending up when I set out that morning. I knew something had to change. This would not have been my first choice, but there was no gun to my head, so on some level, it must have seemed reasonable.

If you go far enough down the rabbit hole you just might come out on the other side!

There really aren't any words to describe my state or the state of affairs at the time, but I am claiming to be a writer, so I will keep digging. Where I was that night was absolutely the last place on Earth I imagined myself being after all that had led up to it. I had been certain my time in institutions and facilities were done and that I had put in enough of whatever was required to sail off into the sunset, as it were. I had more than enough money in the bank at the time to do exactly that for as long as I pleased, yet here I was, about to enter yet another twilight zone and journey down the hall of mirrors. There was absolutely no bone in my body that had any hope about this, and the only reason I was there was that the other options were already known and were on a collision course with all the rocks and hard places I had found myself trapped in. If I possessed the tools at the time to get myself moving, I certainly would have, but this was where the train went off the tracks this time.

What was CAMH like? Well, if there's ever been a loaded question, that one has a full clip—and enough extra ammunition to take out the entire city. It's one of those occasions I've attempted to obliterate from my consciousness as time has gone on, but I shall do my utmost to come up with something.

> "We refused to be what you wanted us to be. We are what
> we are. That's the way it's going to be." – Bob Marley

"So, they build this world on great confusion, to
force on us the devil's illusion." – Bob Marley

My time there can perhaps only be described as surviving an unbelievable situation. Just when you imagine you've seen it all, you haven't.
To call this location a hospital was stretching that word to its very limit.
I don't wish to venture further into dark realms, but I cannot say I was
anything less than shocked at the state of affairs upon being admitted.
Many sections of the unit were in a state of disrepair, there was scant
evidence of any adherence to accessibility standards, the food—and I use
that term very loosely—appeared to be designed to take life as opposed
to support it, there was a general lack of structure, and I am still uncertain
what method of treatment actually took place there other than taking
away people's ability to kill themselves.

I was a veteran of institutions by then, so my expectations weren't
exactly unreasonable. It appeared that the sole motivation of this particular institution was to keep the patients from being a danger to themselves
and provide them no opportunity to continue whatever addiction they
had. They kept the doors locked and you couldn't leave unless you had a
critical reason to go outside. The scene approached what you've seen in
some classic prison films, with the difference being that no crimes had
been committed, as far as I knew. Perhaps my judgements are too harsh
and were coloured by my perspective at that stage—that anything short
of a palace in Beverly Hills would have appeared to me a slum. As I have
said, though, my hesitation in seeking assistance was that I had done this
tour of duty before. I knew the results may well have been worth it, but it
would be no walk in the park. And this sojourn turned out to be a barefoot trek through a jungle freshly infested with poisonous snakes.

There is no you in quit. Well there is a "u" but not you. So quitting is
not an option.

There was a whole different cast of characters in this act. A blessed
collection of misfits (including myself, if you will). This train station
attracted younger passengers, for the most part, who, for various
reasons, had lost the light in their eyes too soon and were now looking
for new ground, as far as I could tell. Though the circumstances were

lifetimes and universes apart, you could say, so was I. This motley crew of wanderers provided the one and only respite from the rocks and hard places. We all somehow managed to cocoon ourselves on a daily basis from the reality around us. The only thing I can compare it to is the festival experiences I described early on—except this time, the only vast, open fields were the stories we shared while searching for ourselves. We would literally spend hours telling the tales of how we had arrived there, as this sort of activity qualified as treatment in this establishment.

This was the bright light shining through the expansive cracks. It renewed my knowledge of serendipity, or as Uncle Jerry Garcia says, "Once in a while, you get shown the light in the strangest of places, if you look at it right." That was the magic of institutionalization: the experiences that could absolutely only happen on the inside, the ones that these or any other words can truly never do justice to—the ones that kept me going. Yet they were also the ones that weren't worth what it took to get them, even though I was eternally grateful at the time. I'm not saying things turned into a joyride—far from it. Those times made the unbearable less so, yet far from pleasant, easy, or remotely similar to the way they'd been anywhere else.

The interactions with what I began to call my CAMH tribe, in effect, became the treatment. Whether they had been prescribed or not, I saw them as the reason I had ended up there. It was medicine for the isolation I'd experienced after the settlement. I don't know if the doctors were aware of this, but that was the point. The official purpose for my stay was determined to be as a bridge while I was on the waiting list for the place that could treat my brain injury. That didn't really seem reasonable in and of itself, but nothing at the time was particularly reasonable—and are any reasons really reasonable? Once again, acceptance had to take over in order for any form of progress to be made. I had been there for approximately a week, and the plan was to be there for at least another.

Once the second week was underway, I was back to my typical position of extension requests. My situation was still far from pleasant or even hopeful, but it did now contain a reasonable amount of purpose. The purpose arose in the form of my passing on my various escapades to the youngsters, which they seemed to have a great appreciation for, as I did for them. I knew this manner of exchange would not be possible on the outside, despite the usual protestations to the contrary. They offered up the same polite hopes for reunification on the outside, but up to now, none have happened and even then, I knew they wouldn't. So, I gave those kids all I had—and perhaps they did, too. They will actually never know how much they did for me, unless they come across this. So it was. So it is.

In between the extended communal moments, there were still issues: waiting to hear about the next destination, other questionable patients who weren't interested in visiting the island commune, living in a room that barely met that definition in many ways—including having no windows and providing no protection from noise at any time. There were other things as well, which, for the benefit of my current progress, I won't recall at this time. But I will tell you they weren't pretty. By this time, I was once again in the steady rhythm of another dance in the twilight zone, so I wasn't exactly pushing my exit. Whatever I can say about the circumstances, they certainly replaced the sterility of regular existence and contained every imaginable element other than boredom.

Any progress I experienced there intertwined and coincided with communication from Ontario Shores in Whitby, Ontario, which was to be the next residence of yours truly. That was always going to be the case—as whatever I had went far beyond CAMH's capacity to handle. CAMH—or that particular branch of it—was meant for standard varieties of madness, such as depression, addiction, violence in various forms, self-abuse, and all versions of anxiety (a condition I'm still not quite clear about, since precisely 100 percent of the planet are afflicted). My malady was a bit more complex. It existed far deeper in the neurological realms and was beyond what any pill could ever handle—at least not one they could provide! What else can be said about CAMH? Everything that happened there was really beyond words. It was beyond challenging, yet it provided camaraderie that was rare (and possibly not even real, since none of us had much choice than to get along). Whatever it was, it was one for the books.

I could have carried on with those "living" room debates with the kids for lifetimes, but my number was up once again. I was definitely road-weary at that point, but you know what they say... the show must go on.

Now, we prepare to turn the page.

CHAPTER 14

Down by the River

There's no one to wait for... They're waiting for you.
The wind in your face shall be at your back.
The colder the wind, the brighter the moon.
The deeper the freeze, the brighter the stars.
The darker the sky, the brighter the stone.
Someone can only take what you're willing to give.

Are we there yet? Exactly how much of his brain did this guy lose? Perhaps he should get back on drugs? These may be some of the question you're asking if you've made it this far. I was also wondering if, through all the twists and turns, I had actually missed the right exit to the location where things began to turn around and all come together. And If there wasn't such a place, I was on the way to Neverneverland once again. Sometimes, it just doesn't make sense. But the single notion that gave life was that there just had to be a reason. That the bright sunlight of Jah was going to break through any minute. I still can't tell you what kept that hope alive, but that's the mystery. I had to continue well into the mystery in order to see that light, though.

What do I mean? I just had to keep taking that one next step, with the absolute knowledge one of them would crack the frozen lake wide open to reveal the pot of gold at the end of this watery rainbow. That made perfect sense, since the river had run dry for so long. This was an effort in the mastery of struggle for no reason at all. Have faith also that the tide will turn.

And turn, mine did.

On the way to wherever, one of the first forks in the road led in a fortunate direction. This one came quite quickly after departing from CAMH. When I first took up residence there and was still completely out of my mind, I was, for lack of a better word, rescued by two friends. I had met them in the midst of an earlier period of madness while attending mindfulness-based meetings. These meetings were rooted in Buddhist philosophy, but borrowed from the twelve-step tradition. I joined the group after somewhat outgrowing my original twelve-step foundation (though I still haven't given it up completely). Through the twists and turns—which were par for the course for anyone involved with me on any level at the time—these two individuals became employed by me as "attendants," if you will.

When something came up that I couldn't handle—say, for example, waking up—they would fill that role, and basically make sure I was functioning to some degree. They assisted with implementing a schedule, which I was not able to follow the majority of the time. When I was admitted at CAMH, they were the first ones I called—and they showed up, thankfully. Through these continued relationships, they connected me with a place called Nature's Retreat, which offered a fusion approach to wellness that employed Native traditions. I took advantage of the opportunity to take a what appeared to be a step back into my real life. This type of thing was routine back before the games began, and though I didn't know exactly what I was doing, I went for it—as a step into the unknown, to get back to the known. This was my first step back into the wild life I knew to be true. For the most part, I was left to wander the vast grounds in the daytime, while in the evening, there would be a combination of ceremony, discussion, and treatment. I communed with the wild nature that surrounded me just outside Toronto. All this was about a million miles from the clinical experiences of the prior years. It really seemed that the shackles were finally being loosened.

I was there for about a week. It all culminated with a personal sweat lodge, which was a true rebirth. I received a call from Ontario Shores near the end of it and left with a real sense of hope. I don't have much contact with the individuals involved these days, but am eternally grateful for that unexpected journey.

It was now some time past the summer of 2015. By then, I had been on the Ontario Shores waiting list for a long enough time to have succumbed to something to a far worse ailment than that which I had been going there for. Even after I had gotten a call from Ontario Shores, it was still an interminable amount of time between then and actual admittance. Most likely due to the effects of that delay, I ended up in yet another facility, this time by the name of the Gerstein Crisis Centre.

Going there must surely have been a sign my ship was coming in. Compared to the last venture, and just about any other manner of health facility I'd been to or heard of, this was absolute Heaven. They had a fantastic downtown residence and transformed it into a refuge for those with some particular struggle or other that didn't require hospitalization. Unbelievable meals, a prime location, a private room, better furnishings than most hotels, and a staff at your beck and call who actually appeared to give a damn. Where had this oasis been a few brief weeks before? *Nothing before its time*, I kept telling myself. But finally, a twist of fate in the right direction. This was surely the result of an unexpected blast of the karmic winds. A true blessing. This provided the impetus for me to carry on to the next essential piece of the puzzle.

Some days after very reluctantly leaving the paradise of the Gerstein Centre, the call came again from Ontario Shores, the call to say that a spot was available should I wish to take it. There was no pondering or debating to be done on this one. I had a day or two to make a choice. You must realize it was getting close to a year since I had gotten onto the waiting list, so it seemed totally unreasonable for there to be no time to make a decision. I also had virtually no idea what I was getting myself into, other than this was to be my last attempt at voluntary clinical intervention. Whatever my position, that was theirs. Take it or leave it, essentially. Rooms there were apparently at a premium, so time was of the essence. Now, pondering is a particularly noteworthy talent of mine—one that has allowed me to produce these pages, in fact. I had further developed this skill though all the prolonged stops on the way to where I found myself then. It would be of no value at this crossroads, though. The chips were on the table, and I guess they called my bluff, since I said that I was in.

The reality was that all my chips were now on the table, which was also a bluff since I held no aces. If I was actually able to get it together enough to make it there, in Whitby, Ontario, roughly an hour from Toronto, my plan was to let them know that unless they were in for the long haul, not to even bother getting started with me. I was going to tell them I knew how this story went: become functional for a while, leave, head back into the world, and not too long after that, do it all over again. No, sir—this time, I had to get to the root of things and find a sustainable existence. Or they could leave me to my own devices. It was time to get off the rollercoaster.

Now, for the issue of actually getting there. I had not left the confines of Toronto for the better part of six years at that point, so it wasn't a simple equation. I was by then essentially institutionalized so seemingly simple, practical matters such as that were something far different to me. This was another moment when the angels came into play. On that occasion, they appeared in the form of my sponsor. On the very day I was meant to be there, he, for no good reason, was available to take me there—and make sure I actually went. You must understand this individual had a full-time job and a family with very young children, so this was far beyond a mere favour from a friend. In hindsight, I know it was divine inspiration making sure I got there, since if I hadn't, I know I wouldn't be here now.

So, after some more debate, the final call was made to hit the road again. To add another twist of preserved lemon, as I do, we were embarking from 341 Bloor Street West, which I still held as an address. I'll leave that to confuse you for a bit, as it did me. I hastily gathered what seemed to be necessary for yet another blind-faith mission. This spot purportedly held the cure for my specific form of optical illusion. The most taxing items to assemble were the remaining shattered fragments of my mind, along with whatever physical essentials made sense for a one-way trip into the deepest, completely un-navigated jungle yet.

This jungle was entitled Ontario Shores Centre for Complex Mental Health Sciences. Complex Mental Health you ask? The simple answer is that this wasn't your garden-variety or McDonald's psychiatric facility. No sir, this was the Siberia of psych. wards. It was for those that all the rest either could not or would not handle.

For the rest of this chapter to make any reasonable sense, you really had to be there. I will have to scour the cosmos to locate the appropriate way to translate what actually transpired in this phase...

Upon arrival at the destination of Ontario Shores the journey was not quite completed. As darkness descended, my hesitation grew. This necessitated further debate with my compadre, in order to make that final, or perhaps, first step. This was not a brief interlude—in fact, a few more hours passed. I'm certain I was now receiving messages from the hospital as to whether or not I was still coming. Nevertheless, we carried on, as this was really a step into the abyss of the unknown, even for an institutional veteran, such as myself, (so was my friend). All the previous stops were simply the regular season on the circuit. The mental health playoffs were now underway! And, for my life, these were the finals!

You never know what you're capable of until you do. Nobody can do everything... except you.

With that, the moment had arrived. My brother, as it was, had a life to return to, as I had one to hopefully reignite. There was also an expiration date on this invitation, 24 hours, to be exact, as memory serves. I began navigating out of the quicksand of hesitation, in the direction of the entrance. Even writing this now brings some unease, but nothing compared to what it was really like that day, which had now drifted into night. They say he who hesitates is lost, and my ally now insisted that the time for that was past, as he accompanied me to the appropriate unit. That he could do this was highly unusual, which you would know, if you have ever treaded on such thin ice. It's usually family only. Perhaps I explained that this really was family, in the truest sense of the word. Or perhaps I was at the point of not giving a damn about such riddles of beaurocracy. But there was nothing usual about this crossroads. We opened the door of no return—there was no turning back now. The intake discussion began with the nurse who greeted us. This evolved into some sort of negotiation, on both parts. I made it abundantly clear, that this was not going to be like the rest. Do or die, literally, on both parts.

Well, there we were, or, more precisely at that point, there I was. I wish I could say I jumped in headfirst, but it would be more accurate to say that only my toes were in the water by that point. There were assurances made that this time would definitely be different, and that they specialized in the treatment that was required, and hadn't been previously available, or prescribed, namely, to treat brain injuries, which were definitely not dealt with on the previous occasions, and if they were, only in passing, or, only in theory, or on paper. They also agreed that it made sense that this was not to be a short-term visit, but a thorough examination of all the issues involved. My main stipulation was to, under no circumstances, be a return visitor. With that, I signed my life away for the umpteenth time. I don't know that there was any paperwork involved, but I was now in. In for exactly what, I still wasn't sure. This definitely was not a typical admission. Ontario Shores, as I was about to discover, was anything but.

I currently doubt that a phenomenon such as a typical psychiatric facility actually exists in the known universe, or any other one, for that matter. All I knew about this one was that it was next to Lake Ontario, and apparently renowned for their particular brand of service. Day had now certainly transformed into night, which, most likely, impacted the admittance process. If it had been the morning, we could have carried on the debates and negotiations for several more rounds or opted for an early discharge! The unit that I was now to call home, for an indeterminate amount of time, was entitled, or perhaps categorized, as neuropsychiatric. This was akin to moving to the penthouse floor of a hotel, compared to where I was coming from. Just a bit more specialized, a bit harder to get into, better amenities, and, quite possibly, a better culinary selection! All kidding aside, Ontario Shores is a cut above other similar establishments, in that, they really do focus on the long-term, and they are one of the few places that are able to treat the more acute and complex variations of mental crisis, a category which I definitely fit at the time.

There we were. Here we are. Another step into yet another abyss. The second point of negotiation centred around my clear, and demonstrated, inability to share a room. Considerably more clearly, this malady is an issue in public hospitals, especially mental ones. This was not a preference, a desire, or a brazen attempt at entitlement. It was an actual need, that had developed over the course of time, for whatever reason. On all previous occasions, after much effort by all parties, a solution was able to be found. I was told that they would seek to do the same here. Without this condition, one can easily gather how the entire effort would be redundant. Moving on, we moved on. Off to the races once again! I believe it was late at night by that time, so the unit must have been quite empty, leaving an opportunity, or a tragic misfortune, to contemplate how this was going to manifest itself. The only possibility that I could focus on at that point, was the one that led directly back to life. I definitely had no notion of exactly how this was going to take place, I just knew that it had to. Everyone involved assured me that they shared the same intention. Hopefully, that would be enough. I have gone on to discover that works alone are not enough, and that it is of far more value, to know, without a shadow of a doubt, WHAT you will do, and not, HOW you will do it.

"The road is made by walking." –Antonio Machado

Enough! Onwards.

This next phase will describe events which may not appear to be possible. Part of the effort here, is to provide evidence of the impossible becoming possible, and then routine. That was precisely the case at Ontario Shores. The initial adjustments were similar to what I experienced in the other places, with the difference being that this one had more extreme cases, so the daily reality went hand in hand with that. A few, and I do emphasize few, of the scenarios which became par for the course, were as follows:

1. Hearing the question, "Am I Alive?", on more than a few occasions, and wondering what a sincerely appropriate answer might be.
2. Attempting to have rational conversations with many who could not be reasonably defined as being "here".
3. Learning how to exist with one set of clothes for an extended period.

4. Navigating a quite restricted system of movement, from the unit to wherever you may be privileged enough to go to for that precious hour, or two, per day, that you may have been granted freedom for.

5. Becoming engrossed in the daily debate on whether or not a more viable living situation had manifested itself.

6. Becoming intimately acquainted with a variety of human dysfunctions, far more than I would have previously imagined to have existed.

7. Becoming well-acquainted with a few who were there as an explanation for their crimes, or as an option to jail.

8. Attending bootcamp, while previously under the impression that I was actually attending a psychiatric facility for treatment of my brain.

9. Going on the journey of adjusting to new medications, which is not quite as humorous as it sounds.

10. Experiencing the joys of extreme constipation, in combination with not having a toilet readily available, on the rare occasions when this issue was resolved, or, when one was available. Finding that it didn't have the industrial capacity that was necessary to contain the contents of said resolutions.

11. Witnessing the variety of situations that can arise when amongst a group of individuals who don't typically have full control over their own faculties.

12. Being denied some of your basic freedoms, due to an occurrence that had nothing to do with you.

13. Enduring my "roommates". I have no judgement of these individuals, but their maladies were far worse/different than mine, such as, apparent schizophrenia, insomnia, inability to control one's own bowels, apparent disregard, or lack of knowledge of, the majority of social norms, amongst a host of others, which I probably can't even pronounce, let alone write. At times, there were four of us in one, less than appropriately sized room. I don't believe I have to go much further to illuminate what challenges this led to.

14. Getting into a fight with a fellow client of the unit. This led to the unique circumstance of becoming MORE injured while in hospital.

15. Navigating the delicate intricacies of interactions with staff. There were many peculiar instances here, including one in which, one of the regulars on the unit, made the point that, "With my income, I didn't need to be there anyway." There was also the suggestion that my brain wasn't attached to my stomach, which was revolutionary news indeed. This all became par for the course. One had to learn to practice not biting the hand that feeds, or to accept the poison.
16. Becoming intimately acquainted with the true nature of "harm reduction", and it's fundamental differences with sobriety. This led to the question of who's harm was the practice really reducing?
17. Becoming familiar with the intricacies of the restrictive, and some-what "prison-like" systems.
18. Observing the varied and complex scenarios which would unfold daily, on what I came to refer to as, "the patio".
19. Experiencing the "private room", which was anything but.
20. Becoming acquainted, on various levels, with some of the more "complex" clientele.
21. Noting the unique matriarchy which existed throughout the facility. From my observation, the resounding majority of the staff were female, while the reverse was true with the doctors.

Again, I include such descriptions, not for pity, or even sympathy, but to show the stark reality of what became, effectively, a bootcamp. At each one of these crossroads, the only choice was radical acceptance. No fences to sit on in this locale. Either go backwards, into a quicksand of desperation, or, headlong into an unknown, of some potential. With that, the path was evermore clear. I then had to go along with absolutely every opportunity that this locale provided.

Separate and apart from stepping over these minefields, was the even more tangible, and pressing matter, of getting on with creating an every-day life, as, once again, bootcamp is only a temporary vacation. What do I mean by bootcamp? Well, that's what life turned into during this chapter. There was no choice in it: either I became like the others or I came out the other side, a better person. That was the basic scene at Ontario Shores, Neuropsychiatry Ward.

Looking at things with these eyes, many revealed themselves. I pressed on, with no regard for difficulty or consequence. I uncovered a school, a perfect A.A. meeting, various vocational classes, physiotherapy, a fantastic gym, yoga classes, music therapy, a library, equipped with a master librarian, a spectacular outdoor setting, and the lake! The lake was a tipping point. That was where the cup started to overflow with new fire, rising from the ashes of the past. I don't exactly know how that happens, but you don't have to either, just know that it does. More to come on the lake. You never know what you can do until you do. And now that I did, I certainly did. At a certain point of this juncture, I began a further personal undertaking of the science of human success. I delved further into the likes of Robbins, Dyer, Coello, Pirsig, Chopra, Siddartha, Nietzsche, Tolle, amongst many others in the realm of self-mastery. This was interspersed with my continuous reverence for the likes of Marley, Tosh, Miles, 'Trane, Hendrix, Osho, and a new light on the horizon, Sharma. I also had my mentors on this plane, who took the form of the many who serendipitously crossed my path, at precisely the right moment. Most continue to be there. It all led to the discovery that we are all teaching each other constantly, whether consciously or not.

These were the days. Those days started out as interminable lifetimes, then morphed into collective moments, ultimately blending into months of progress. These got to the point of being granted "passes" on the weekend, even though I never have, and don't plan to ever, require, protection from myself, at least not according to the clinical definition.

The most striking, and irrefutable evidence of my progress is the fact that I'm still here. Hopefully, you have gathered that there was ample reason for that not to be so. By my own hand, or otherwise. Even though I've laid it all out for you, warts and all, I'm still not quite sure how that's the case. Exactly how I'm able to pass on wise words, when there was a time when I was at a great loss to find any at all? How am I able to teach writing, when I'm not certain from whence it came? Then there's the mystery of not being able to communicate with a single soul for months, and now I will purposely go to great lengths to do just that for the briefest of moments?

CHAPTER 15

The Juice Is Worth the Juice

Life is my full-time gig. By that I mean it takes the maximum of my energy to participate in life on a functional level due to all the complications I have mentioned. Anything beyond that, such as this miracle in your hands currently is gravy. It is my hope for you that every moment in which there is no struggle for existence that you use it as a struggle for excellence. So, what for me is gravy shall for you be your meal, if you so require, if you so desire. Do the opposite of what is expected. Don't go for the comfort but rather the struggle. My struggle has turned out to be showing up for life itself so I encourage you to go far past me. And let me tell you, you can. Get to the stars so I can here the story. If you don't have a particular struggle, I would recommend that as your struggle.

I must emphasize here that I am in no way officially qualified to pass on any of this. As a result, I don't wish for you to take my word for it. Go out there and put it to the test. Please prove that I'm full of shit, because on many levels I am. Though I am definitely not when I say that if someone had put this challenge before me way back when, I would have turned it down. No way, not possible. If you've come this far, you may be willing to trust it when I say that nothing can break you if you don't allow it. Absolutely everything that I never believed I could be, I now know to be possible. Every path that I purposely avoided, is now part of the regular route.

What's a typical day now? Well, I attempt not to do or be anything typical at any time, but there are everyday realities. One of those realities is the acceptance of pain, real physical pain. This has arisen, to the best of my knowledge, from the spinal cord injury. This is neuropathic, and clinically referred to as spasticity. The most literal way I can describe this is having constant stiffness, of what the majority would consider to be the exteme variety. I believe this would cause most to stop their plan for that day. However, I have no choice in this. It's not going away, and there is no cure. There is a pill for it, but the consequence of those are worse than the pain. The average day for me, may be what it's like for you to do your hardest and most complete workout of the day, where you push yourself past your perceived limit. I'm highlighting this in order to suggest that you do that everyday. I have had to condition myself to do that, in order to have any quality of life at all. If you can harness this, you will be running up Everest in no time! The daily mental reality of a brain injury? I would have to send you my psychiatrist's notes to properly explain that one. The short answer is that this condition has fostered the ability to only focus on the beneficial aspects of my consciousness, at all times. This has been akin to walking through minefields constantly, or perhaps learning how to make feces smell like roses. This level of focus has allowed *me* to simply participate in life—if *you* can master this same focus, the sky will be your starting point.

Here's what I can offer:

Get outside. Get inside. Get out of yourself. Get into yourself to get out of yourself. Get out of the city. Get out of the lies. Get out of the house. Get out of the car. Get out of the driver's seat. Get out of the line. Get out of line. Get out of the problem. Get out of the way. Get out of your way. Get in the way. Just get out. Get off the throne. Get on the throne. Get out of debt. Get out of the danger. Get out of breath. Take another. Get out of it. Get into it. Get into it. Get into it. Get into it. Get into it. Into it. Intuit. Get going. Get to it. Get through it. Get what you've got to get. Leave what you must leave. Leave. Leaf. Leave leaves. Leave the leaves. Get on with it. Get over it. Get under it. Get inside it. Get away from it. Get away. Get there. Get here. Get hair. Get hare. Leave here. Leaf hare. Get to give. Yet to give. Yet to live. Live and let live. Live and let give. Give up. Get up. Stand up. Stay up. Stand down. Get down. Haw far down. Get a grip. Lose your grip. Lose yourself. Find yourself.

Find someone. Lose someone. Loose someone. Get out. While you still can. Get out of your mind. Now. While you still can.

CHAPTER 16

To Whom it May Still Concern

My concern is still you, as I hope it is still yours. Well, here we are, we are still here, and that's all it will ever be. Be still here, still be here. I've made it to tell the tale. What will your story be. Still may your story be. I may not tell another. Maybe I'm waiting on yours? Perhaps you're waiting for yours? Please don't wait for me, I'm not the best at being on time. But it's the right time for you. It always has been. Stop waiting.

I've given you all I can here. Many may say "What more can I ask for?". You can always ask for more, and you may certainly get it; in fact, it's the only way to get it. It just may not be from me, on this particular occasion. Ask it of yourself, you can always deliver on time. I've given you facts here, without compromise, to the best of my recollection. It may not have been typically perfect, but it was what it was, and it is what it is. I gave a full effort in the area of literary standard, but may have erred, from time to time, in favour of effect. The effect which I hoped for was inspiration. So, if logic was lacking, now you know why. I don't claim to be an expert on anything other than what I saw with my own two eyes. I received several lifetimes worth of education during the 8 or so years that led to this work. I'm estimating that 8 years, the amount of time that it took to get from the "accident" to a point of progress that I determined to be noteworthy, and of potential benefit to others. I have left out a few details, only because I have discovered that I am not a fan of courtrooms, no matter which side of the case I am on. If it was up to me, it would all be here. But what use would I be to anyone, if I could barely take care of myself? What real freedoms could I comment on, if I had so few myself? You see, what I desire for you is complete freedom, all of them, inside and out, black and white, even the greys, the sacred and the profane, all and none, everything and nothing. You've heard some of that before. On the occasions that I repeat myself, it's for the repeated effect of driving home the point that this life is hours, and yours alone.

I owe you a great debt. A debt of gratitude. Gratitude for having come this far. And for embarking on the journey in the first place. This certainly was not a pleasure cruise, it was more of an expedition through torturous waters, with no view of the shore. If you didn't have the nature of a surfer, you would not still be here. For that, I am eternally grateful. You have also allowed for this work to reside beyond the realms of my own mind. For a new life to be born. For a new purpose to arise. Writing this has been ultimate therapy for me. To be able to go from having a great fear of my own toilet, to the possibility of motivating others, has been nothing less than a revelation. The road to here may not have been exactly straight, some of that was by design, some was faulty navigation on my part, but the intention was always to stay the course. And that you did, and I thank you for not switching lanes when the writing may have. This truly was my blood and sweat, and, hopefully, not too many tears, hence the mess. I truly was a lone sailor, in stormy seas here. This is my first book, and the topic was treacherous—thanks for the trust.

I'm currently on a trip to Niagara Falls to attend a brain injury conference. This is part of my reality these days. This is also a voyage of redemption. How so, you might ask? Well, the first time I came to this event, back around 2016, I was unable to book a room for myself, had to completely rely on others to get there, and only played the role of observer, for the duration of it. This time around, I registered as part of the event, had my own necessary credit cards to book a room, was able to qualify for the survivor's rate, and got there completely on my own, with no special accommodations with regard to transportation. All the way on the GO train, from Whitby to Niagara Falls for me! A roughly three-and-a-half-hour journey. Of greater note, on this occasion, I was able to mingle with many that I have come to know over the years, in various capacities, as opposed to simply mingling, or waiting for the evening's events. It was as if I was working there myself. I suppose you could say that I was, as the topic of this book came up frequently. I should also mention that I was barely able to get dressed the last time, while this time a stranger started a conversation by asking where I got my shoes! All this may seem like par for the course, but as you now know, in this story, there is no such thing. All of these were great victories, which would not have been predicted by most, and at times, not even by me.

CHAPTER 17

When There's Nothing Left to Say, It's Time to Move On

We are approaching that point.

Pain in the morning is training for the evening. Everyone is everything.

Love isn't enough, but you are. You're here to discover yourself.

The time is right, right is the time. The right time is now, now is the right time.

Get on with it or move on. You were meant for this. Keep your head in the clouds. You are the force. Use your self.

All paths contain stones. Choose wisely. Every road contains detours, but only one doesn't go in circles.

Today is the day. The day is today. Forwards. Backwards. Backwards. Forwards. Get to it. To it, get. Get it? Get it.

The wise man stands alone. The fool follows... Socialized, social lies, so-called lies. Vocalize.

So, would I change anything? It's not currently an option—so, in a word, no. Keep moving on from the fantasy to the reality, which is the fantasy. Chase the shadow and chase forever. Find yourself and the chase is over. No need to chase the truth—it was always waiting for you.

Everyone can do everything, and you can certainly do more than something. You can and you did. As there is a shade of blue in the space between the keys, so are you greater than the sum of your parts.

The choice is yours. Is the choice yours? Yours is the choice. Is yours the choice? Choice, is this yours? Choice, this is yours. Choice, yours, this is.

There is no end. Or any beginning.

This it is. This is it. This is it. This it is. Is this it? It, this is. This is it. Is this it?

Printed in the USA
CPSIA information can be obtained
at www.ICGtesting.com
JSHW020927091224
74885JS00001B/1/J